The Holy Spirit:
Purpose, Power and Presence

Dr. Don T. Phillips

Pastor Lupe Gallardo

"The Holy Spirit: Purpose, Power and Presence," by Don T. Phillips and Lupe Gallardo. ISBN 978-1-63868-194-6.

Published 2025 by Virtualbookworm.com Publishing Inc., P.O. Box 9949, College Station, TX 77845, US. Copyright ©2025 Don T. Phillips.

All rights reserved. No part of this publication may be reproduced, stored in a retrieval system, or transmitted in any form or by any means, electronic, mechanical, recording or otherwise, without the prior written permission of Don T. Phillips.

Dedication

This book is Dedicated to every member of:

Faith Outreach Christian Center

Navasota, Texas

May they all find Peace, Happiness, and Salvation in our Lord Jesus Christ

It is also dedicated to our life-long partners in Christ

Candyce J Phillips

Mary Hellen Gallardo

Preface

This book is a compilation of sermon and bible study notes which was offered to the congregation of the Faith Outreach Christian Center in Navasota, Texas. The purpose was a multi-month study on the Holy Spirit. During this study, it was discovered that even though the Holy Spirit is recognized as a part of the Holy Trinity… Father-Son-Holy Spirit… the critical part that the Holy Spirit plays in Salvation and ministry of every Christian is often poorly understood and recognized.

Every Christian is aware that salvation is offered to every Jew and Gentile by *faith* and *grace*. The issue of sin was settled forever by Jesus Christ on the Cross of Calvary. The sacrificial death and the blood that was shed by our Lord and Savior Jesus Christ on the Cross of Calvary was the final and complete payment for the sins of man… Past, Present and Future. Because Jesus Christ paid the ultimate price for all sin, we can now stand justified before the Throne of God. When Jesus Christ died on the Cross, the Old Covenant which was based upon works under the Law was finished… The Levitical priesthood was finished… Temple sacrifices which only atoned for sin was finished… and a New Covenant was ratified by Christ based upon *faith*… salvation was offered by *Grace* to all who would truly believe upon our Lord and Savior: Jesus Christ. Salvation by faith and grace was offered first to the Jews on the Feast of Pentecost 50 days after Christ rose from the grave. After the Jewish spiritual leaders rejected Christ and stoned Steven; God offered salvation by faith to both Jews and Gentiles. Saul of Tarsus (Paul) was chosen by God to define how either Jew or Gentile could be saved and live a life in Christ under this *New Covenant*. As our (Gentiles) *seal* and *guarantee*, Paul wrote that the Holy Spirit would *proceed* from God the

Father at the request of Jesus Christ to anyone who would commit their life on this earth to serve Jesus Christ. This is accomplished by being Born-again. This Gift is not automatically given to everyone who professes to be a Christian; You must be Born-again.

During His last hours here upon this earth, Christ promised:

[15] *If ye love me, keep my commandments.*
[16] *And I will pray the Father, and he shall give you another Comforter, that he may abide with you forever;*
[17] *Even the Spirit of truth; whom the world cannot receive, because it sees him not, neither knoweth him: but ye know him; for he dwelleth with you, and shall be in you.*
[18] *I will not leave you comfortless: I will come to you*
John 14: 15-18

This is a tremendous promise: Jesus told His apostles and disciples that after His death He would ask the Father to send them the *Holy Spirit*. This was *before* Paul was chosen to reveal the Mystery of the New Covenant: salvation would be offered by faith to Jews and Gentiles alike. Paul wrote 13 Epistles to which explained how to be saved and live a new life in Jesus Christ under the New Covenant.

Salvation is now offered by *faith* and is appropriated by *grace*. Once a person believes in faith that Jesus Christ was the Son of God; He died for our sins on the Cross of Calvary; was dead, buried and resurrected, and is now seated on the Throne of God with His Father… something miraculous happens to that person. At the instant of true surrender and faith, that person is *Born-again*. That person dies to a sinful world, receives the **Gift of the Holy Spirit**, and is **baptized by the Holy Spirit** into the Body of Christ. This cannot take place in a believer's life unless that person is ***Born-again***. When a person yields his/her life to Christ that person receives the Gift of the Holy Spirit. The Holy Spirit comes to live inside man and help that person to fulfill John 14:12. The Holy Spirit will bring 9 Gifts of the Holy Spirit to live a new life in Christ. This is being Born-again, and it will be verified from scripture that salvation is by faith, and it is through faith that a person is Born-again. We will show that a person must be Born-again to enter the Kingdom of Heaven. What are the consequences of not being Born-again? Jesus said:

[19] *Every tree that bringeth not forth good fruit is hewn down, and cast into the fire.*
[20] *Wherefore by their fruits ye shall know them.*
[21] *Not everyone that saith unto me, Lord, Lord, shall enter into the kingdom of heaven; but he that doeth the will of my Father which is in heaven.*
[22] *Many will say to me in that day, Lord, Lord, have we not prophesied in thy name? and in thy name have cast out devils? and in thy name done many wonderful works?*
[23] *And then will I profess unto them, I never knew you: depart from me, ye that work iniquity* Matthew 7: 19-23

What does all of this mean? Matthew 7: 19-20 clearly states that every Christian is typed as a *tree*, and if that tree does not produce *good fruit*, it will be cast into *fire* and *burned*. if a person is to be a Christian, they *must* carry on the works of Jesus Christ.

Verily, verily, I say unto you, **He that believeth on me**, *the works that I do shall he do also; and greater works than these shall he do; because I go unto my Father* John 14:12

Not everyone who says: *Lord, Lord, shall enter into the kingdom of heaven.* The words of Jesus in John 14:12–14 bear directly on your life and our life together in these last days. What they say is that all of us who believe in Jesus will carry on with his work, and in some wonderful way, do something greater than the works of Jesus. How can this possibly be accomplished? The *power* and *ability* to fulfill this prophecy comes from Jesus Christ and God the Father by the *Holy Spirit*. This book will explain these concepts and the role of the Holy Spirit in both the Old and New Testaments.

Chapter 1 **Introduction**
Chapter 1 is an introduction to the basic concept and roles of the Holy Spirit.

Chapter 2 **The Holy Spirit in the Old Testament**
Chapter 2 presents how God used the Holy spirit in the Old Testament.

Chapter 3 **The Holy Spirit in the New Testament**
Chapter 3 is a summary of how God uses the Holy Spirit in the New Testament. What it means to be Born-again will be discussed: Gifts of the Holy Spirit, their definition and power.

Chapter 4 **The Manifestation of the Holy Spirit**
Chapter 4 discusses how the gifts are allocated and used.

Chapter 5 **Live and be Led by the Spirit**
Chapter 5 is a partial list of what should be recognized as necessary to live and be led by the Holy Spirit.

Don T. Phillips
Lupe Gallardo
Spring, 2025

Table of Contents

Chapter 1 The Holy Spirit 1

    Role of the Holy Spirit 8

        Old Testament 8

        New Testament 9

    Evidence of the Holy Spirit 9

    Manifestation of the Holy Spirit 14

    Baptism of the Holy Spirit 16

    Personification of the Holy Spirit 17

    Purpose of the Holy Spirit 19

    Prescence of the Holy Spirit 20

    Power of the Holy Spirit 22

    Gifts of the Holy Spirit 24

    Fruits of the Holy Spirit 26

Chapter 2 The Holy Spirit in the Old Testament 29

    Gifts of the Holy Spirit in Old Testament 38

Chapter 3 The Holy Spirit in the New Testament 44

    The *Day of Pentecost* 51

    The *Holy Spirit* and *Salvation* 55

    The *Gift* of the Holy Spirit 63

The *Prescence* of the Holy Spirit..63

The *Purpose* of the Holy Spirit 65

The *Power* of the Holy Spirit 69

Baptism by the Holy Spirit 70

Baptism of the Holy Spirit 71

Gifts of the Holy Spirit 74

    General *Gifts* 76

    Power *Gifts* 78

Using the Gifts 86

Fruits of the Holy Spirit...88

Diversity of Gifts: *Old Testament vs New Testament* 90

Summary...91

Chapter 4 **Evidence of the Holy Spirit** 94

    Gift of the Holy Spirit 94

    Manifestation of the Holy Spirit 98

    Indwelling of the Holy Spirit.. 101

    Infilling of the Holy Spirit 108

    Conviction of the Holy Spirit.. 112

    Can One *Lose* the Holy Spirit? 113

    Summary 122

Chapter 5 **Live and be Led by the Spirit** 123

Justification 124

Sanctification 124

Glorification..125

Righteousness..126

Born-again: A New Creature in Jesus Christ 127

Walking in the Spirit..128

Praying in the Spirit 130

Living in the Spirit...130

Witnessing in the Spirit 132

Being Led by the Spirit..133

Bibliography 136

Chapter 1

The Holy Spirit

The original *Holy Scriptures* were written in three different languages. The *Old Testament* was written in Aramaic and Hebrew, and the New Testament was written in Greek. In the Old Testament the word *ruwach* in both Hebrew and Aramaic is translated as *Spirit*, and in the New Testament the Greek word *pneuma* is translated Spirit 133 times and spirit 153 times. *Pneuma* is distinctly associated with the *Spirit* of God, as opposed to the *spirit* which is either another spirit other than God or part of a person's design … Body, Soul, and spirit (Lower Case). The phrase Holy Spirit is used in only two verses in the Old Testament, and only four times in the New Testament (once by Luke and 3 times by Paul).

The *Holy Spirit* can best be defined by recognizing its position and role as related to God the Father and His Son, Jesus Christ. The Holy Spirit is the 3rd person in the divine triune of Father, Son, and the Holy Ghost.

The word *Trinity* comes from the Latin word *trinus,* which means threefold. The Holy Trinity involves *the Father*, *the Son,* and *the Holy Spirit*. There are two fundamental, core beliefs that define the relationship between these three Spirit beings. (1) There is one God who exists in three different persons: God the Father…God the Son…and God the Holy Spirit. They are inseparable and knowing one is to know all three (2) There is only one sovereign and eternal God who exists as part of a triumvirate with God the Son and God the Holy Spirit, but collectively they are not a single God. All three are separate manifestations who are one in agreement, thought, purpose and belief with God the Father. These three are eternal and consubstantial persons (the Father, the Son, and the Holy Spirit).

The term *Trinity* does not appear anywhere in either the Latin, Hebrew, Greek or King James Version of the Holy Bible. There is no Old Testament specific identification of a triune God, and The New Testament contains no explicit trinitarian doctrine. However, many Christian theologians, apologists, and philosophers hold that the doctrine can be inferred from what the full council of Holy Scripture does teach about God. They also admit that a single, triune Godhead was a product of tradition that evolved over 300 years after the death of Jesus Christ. The 1st major statement of faith concerning Jesus Christ and His relationship to God the Father was called **Arianism**: a statement of faith first proposed by Arius of Alexandria that declared Christ was not always present with God, but a spiritual being created by God in the dateless past. It surfaced early in the 4th century by the Alexandrian presbyter called *Arius* and became a popular belief throughout much of the Eastern and Western Roman empires. Arianism divided the Catholic faith into two different camps: One believed that Jesus was created by God along with the Holy spirit and the other group believed that Jesus Christ was always present with God as a co-equal deity. It was not until after years of debate that the concept of the *Trinity* was formally addressed by the Roman Catholic Church at the *First Council of Nicaea* in 325 AD. It was an attempt to articulate Christianity's belief in the oneness of God and the relationship between God the Father and the Son Jesus Christ. Not much was determined by a group of 30 catholic theologians who met in Constantinople, except the following belief was introduced as Catholic faith: The council condemned Arius and, with reluctance on the part of some, incorporated the non-scriptural word *homoousios* (of one substance) into a creed to signify the absolute equality of the Son with the Father. The Holy Spirit was not debated until the Council was almost over, but it was adopted as Catholic doctrine that the Holy Spirit always existed in an intimate relationship with God the Father and God the Son A main theological edict from this meeting was that The Council decreed that there was an eternal Godhead of one sovereign God in three persons: Father, Son, and Holy Spirit each of which were created as three independent Gods with equal status and knowledge. This Triune Godhead was called the *Trinity*.

The Holy Triune Godhead that became known as the *Trinity* was not a serious theological issue until over 300 years had elapsed since Jesus Christ was crucified in 30 AD. After the *First Council of Nicaea* was held in 325 AD, the concept of a Trinity was only partly settled and continued to be hotly debated until it was finally settled at the *Second Council of Nicaea* in 787 AD. The definition and deity of the Holy Trinity was such a divisive issue, that it was largely responsible for a split of the Roman Catholic religion into the Roman Catholic and Eastern Orthodox Catholic Church in 1054 AD.

It is important to understand the concept of the Holy Trinity that the Catholic church established as doctrine in the 4th and 8th century AD. The official doctrine of the Trinity as defined by the Catholic Church was illustrated as shown on the right.

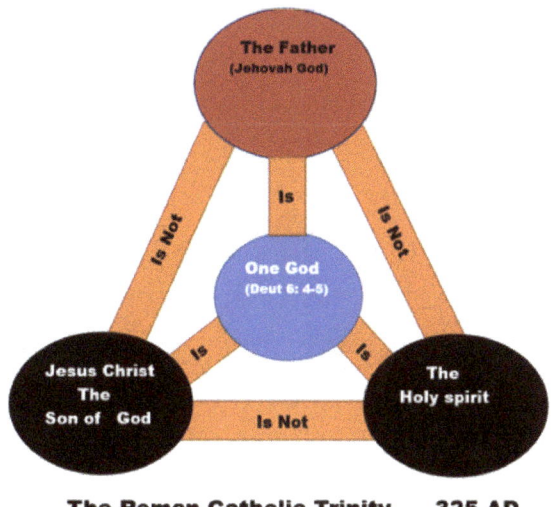

The Roman Catholic Trinity   325 AD

The following is an explanation of the Roman Catholic belief concerning the Holy Trinity.

If you were to ask each Person in the Trinity, "Who are you?" each person would answer something differently: "I am the Father;" "I am the Son;" "I am the Holy Spirit." If you were to ask each Person,

"Are you supreme deity"? you would get the same answer from each Person: "I am God." Not, "I am a God". Each divine Person in the triune godhead, while not identical to the other divine Persons, is one with the other two divine Persons and each is fully God.

The word that is used to describe this doctrine by the Catholic Church in the *Nicene Creed* is *consubstantial*. The Nicene Creed, written at the Council of Nicea in 325 and revised at the Council of Constantinople in 381, was the result of the Church's continued thinking about the Trinity. While we say in the Nicene Creed that the Son is consubstantial with the Father, it is also true that the Spirit is consubstantial with the Father and the Son.
(https://www.aboutcatholics.com/beliefs/the-trinity/

The earliest Christians were Jewish believers. As Jews, they believed that there is only one God and that this God is *YHWH;* the God of Abraham, Isaac, and Jacob. He alone is omnipresent, omniscient, and omnipotent. It is important to note that the early Christians continued to affirm their belief in one God, but they also confessed belief that the Father and the Son both existed as deity.

- God is all-powerful
- God is all-present
- God is all-knowing
- Only one God exists

This was the setting in which the doctrine of the Trinity became an issue to those 1st Century Jews who converted to Christianity. As Jews and Gentiles both became 1st century Christians, the New Testament gospels of Matthew, Mark, Luke, and John emerged which faithfully recorded the message of reconciliation and salvation to the Jews. The *Mystery* of salvation by faith and grace was not fully understood until 13 epistles written by the apostle Paul revealed the mystery of salvation by faith to Jews and Gentiles alike. The words which Jesus spoke to all sinners were as a compassionate and loving father would speak to one of his own sons. His actions clearly revealed that He was the Son of God. After His crucifixion and resurrection, the spiritual and physical encounter with the resurrected Jesus was so profound that the Jews began to worship Jesus as God. But then someone said: *Are you proposing that Jesus Christ was identical to God the Father?* This would be blasphemy and the answer would be *No*, but in their minds, Jesus was God in the second person and was coequal to God. He would not be the Father God, but identical in all ways. Jesus clearly spoke to God as his heavenly Father and commanded us to do the same. To an *orthodox* Jew, Jesus Christ was not identical to God the Father and to say He was would be blasphemy and heretic. This is the Roman Catholic explanation of the Holy Trinity, and if it seems to be confusing… that is because it is. The Holy scriptures clearly reveal that both Jesus Christ and the Holy Spirit *proceeded* from Jehovah God. (John 8:42, John 15:26). Fifty days after His resurrection on the Day of Pentecost the Holy Spirit fell upon around 3,000 new Jewish converts (Acts 2:41), just as John the Baptizer had promised 3.5 years earlier at His baptism of Christ (Matthew 3: 11-12). This was also prophesied by the Prophet Isaiah (Isaiah 12). The experience that these Jewish believers and all other Jews and Gentiles afterward had with the Holy Spirit was powerful and promised by Jesus Christ from the Father, and so these new believers began to also acknowledge the Holt Spirit as a 3rd person coequal to God, but for reasons previously stated He was not God. The Holy Spirit, which is sent to all born-again believers, is neither God the Father or God the Son but he is God in the 3rd person.

Although the term *Holy Trinity* is not found in the Holy Scriptures, the concept of a 3-person Godhead is clearly revealed in the New Testament. The first time that the three are used together is in Matthew 28:19. Jesus Christ had already risen from the grave, and He met with His apostles and disciples on a mountain in Galilee. He commanded them to go unto all the world: *teaching all nations and baptizing converts in the name of the Father, Son, and Holy Spirit*. The composition of the Holy Trinity cannot be fully comprehended, but each of the 3 members exist as a functional member of the nature and will of God the Father. Each member of the Godhead (Father-Son-Holy Spirit) are unique individuals with specific characteristics. Each is identified as God but neither the Holy Spirit or the Son Jesus Christ are fully God. The authors suggest that the Holy Trinity is compose of only one sovereign God, who is manifested in two other persons (Jesus Christ, and the Holy Spirit) which exist to carry out His divine will. They are one in purpose and are always in agreement but they are three distinct persons. Each person of the Trinity relates to the others in intimate communion, love, and submission within the Godhead (Matthew 28:19, John 14:26, 2 Corinthians 13:14), but there is only one supreme God who is omniscient, omnipresent, and omnibenevolent. This relational diagram reflects the belief of the authors concerning the Holy Trinity.

This assumption becomes a near certainty when one considers the relationship under the New Covenant between God the Father, God the Son, and God the Holy Spirit. The Holy Scriptures assert that both the Holy Spirit and Jesus Christ *proceeds* or is sent from the Father.

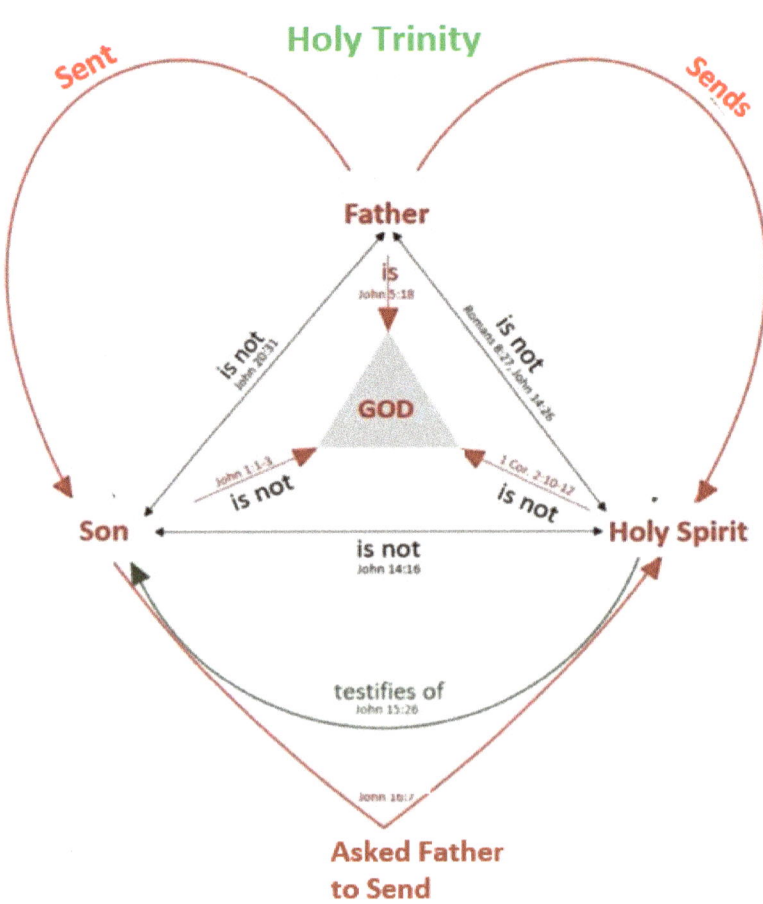

*Jesus said unto them, If God were your Father, ye would love me: for I **proceed**ed forth and came from God; neither came I*

of myself, but he sent me   John 8:42

*But when the Comforter is come, whom I will send unto you from the Father, even the Spirit of truth, which **proceeds from the Father**, he shall testify of me*   John 15:26

Jesus Christ was God incarnate in the body of a man. The spirit part of Jesus Christ always existed. As previously noted, in the Old Testament He was known as *The Word*.

*In the beginning was the Word, and the Word was with God, and **the Word was God**.*   John 1:1

The Holy Spirit also always existed. In the Old Testament: He was known as the *Spirit of God*, *Gods Spirit* or simply the *Spirit*. In the New Testament, the term *Spirit*, *Holy Ghost*, and *Holy Spirit* are used. Jesus Christ said that the Holy Ghost is our *comforter*, and Paul spoke of the Holy Ghost as the *seal* of our salvation.

*But the **Comforter**, **which is the Holy Ghost**, whom **the Father will send** in my name, he shall teach you all things, and bring all things to your remembrance, whatsoever I have said unto you*   John 14:26

*In whom ye also trusted, after that ye heard the word of truth, the gospel of your salvation: in whom also after that ye believed, ye were **sealed with that Holy Spirit of promise***   Ephesians 1:13

Jesus Christ left His spiritual existence in heaven to preach redemption and forgive all sins by His sacrificial death on the Cross of Calvary. If Jesus Christ was fully 100% God as some teach, why would He have to ask God the Father to send to all New Covenant believers the Holy Spirit? God is held by all Jews to be the supreme ruler of the universe and in omniscient, omnipresent, and omnipotent. In Matthew 1:20, the Holy Scriptures reveal that Jesus Christ was *conceived* by the Holy Spirit as the Son of God. The Holy Spirit descended upon the virgin

Mary and she conceived the Messiah. *Should we believe that God the Father sent Himself to birth a son that was Himself?* When Jesus was on the cross and was near death, He cried out to the Father to take this cup (of suffering) from Him. *Was Jesus praying to Himself?*

The only logical conclusion is that both the Holy Spirit and Jesus Christ (who now sits next to His Father on the Father's throne) are both in total agreement and of one mind and one accord with the Father, but they are not all 100 % God. The Holy Trinity are all 3 different persons, and Jesus Christ and the Holy Ghost have unique positions, authority, and responsibilities as part of the eternal Godhead. Belief in one God (*monotheism*) is central to many religious sects. Judaism teaches that God is the only being who should be worshiped and praised.

Role of The Holy Spirit

The *Holy Spirit* is sent to each born-again believer to support the ministry of Christ to which that individual was called. The *Holy Spirit* in the Old Testament was a special gift from God to only a *selected* number of those He called for a specific purpose.

Old Testament

A *Creative Force*... Genesis 1: 1-2, Job 33:4, Psalms 104:30

A *Source of Power*...David and Goliath

A *Source of Strength*... Sampson (Judges 14:6, Judges 15:4)

A *Source of Creativity*... Bezalel, Oholiab

A *Source of Wisdom and Knowledge*... King Saul, King David, King Solomon (Numbers 11:17)

A *Teacher and a Source of understanding*... Job 32:8, Psalms 143:10

Leadership and Military Wisdom… Moses, Joshua, Othniel, Gideon

Note that these attributes in the Old Testament are directly related to ruling or Military prowess.

New Testament

Every Christian today lives in the *Age of Faith and Grace*. In the New Testament, the Holy Spirit is given to *every* Born-again believer to give them special gifts of spirituality and ministry.

A *Comforter*…. John 14:16, John 14:26, John 15:16, John 16:7

Spiritual Inspiration for All Holy Scripture…. II Peter 1:21

Condemn the World of Sin… John 16: 7-11

Defender of the Truth…. John 16:13

To *Glorify* Jesus Christ…. John 16:14

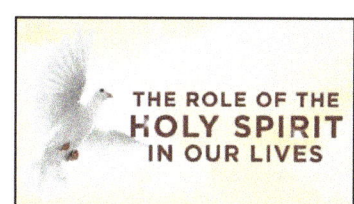

He is our *Advocate*…. I John 2:1

He is our *Comforter*…. John 14:1

He will *Teach* us all things…. John 14:2

He is the *Seal* of Our Redemption… II Corinthians 12:2, Ephesians 2: 8-9

These gifts are more closely aligned with saving souls to Christ under the New Covenant.

Evidence of the Holy Spirit

The Holy Bible is quite clear that the Holy Spirit is a gift from God to everyone who receives salvation and believes *upon* Jesus Christ, *who* He is, and *what* He has done. The question before us is: *When does a person become a true believer?* It is the steadfast belief of these authors that simply saying that *I believe*, is not sufficient to receive the gift of the Holy Spirit. Christ said:

Not everyone that saith unto me, Lord, Lord, shall enter into the kingdom of heaven; but he that doeth the will of my Father which is in heaven   Matthew 7:27

> A recent study found that "huge proportions of people" associated with churches whose official doctrine says eternal salvation comes only from embracing Jesus Christ as savior "believe that a person can qualify for Heaven by being or doing good" (Cultural Research Center at Arizona Christian University). This includes close to half of all adults associated with Pentecostal (46%), mainline Protestant (44%), and evangelical (41%) churches. A much larger share of Catholics (70%) embrace that point of view. In contrast, a minority of adults (46%) who describe themselves as "Christian" expect to experience eternal salvation only because of their confession of sin and acceptance of Christ as their savior.

Recent scholarly investigations reveal that while this is an astounding result for "Christians", things might be worse than imagined.

> A second survey revealed that **one third** of senior pastors agree that: "A person who is generally good, or does enough good things for others, can earn a place in Heaven." This study, also conducted by the Cultural Research Center (CRC), was from a nationwide study of 1,000 pastors over several denominations, and was compiled from February 2022 to March 2022. Aside from the belief that good works can get someone to Heaven, a third or more of senior pastors also believe that determining moral truth is up to each individual, sexual relations between unmarried individuals are acceptable, and that reincarnation is a real possibility.

These studies which were conducted among Christians are both startling and revealing. It is evident that many pastors and Christian church leaders do not believe the Word of God and choose to yield to modern social pressures.

Both coauthors of this book regularly ask the following question when talking to people of all denominations. It is an excellent way to "break the ice."

If you were to die today, would you go to heaven?

The wide range of answers which are given and/or the discourse which might follow is astounding: Only a small percentage answer; YES.

The question which prompted this discourse was: *When does one receive the Holy Spirit?* The above observations and how a person might answer the posed question is directly related to the answer. It has consistently been proposed and supported by Biblical Truth that one cannot be saved without receiving the Holy Spirit, and the Holy Spirit is a gift from God when one is saved and gives his life to Christ. This life-changing experience is called being *Born-again*. Jesus Christ said without any controversy or misunderstanding:

Jesus answered and said unto him: Verily, verily, I say unto thee: Except a man be Born again, he cannot see the kingdom of God   John 3:3

The Apostle John said without any controversy or misunderstanding.

Marvel not that I said unto thee: Ye must be Born again   John 3:7

The Apostle Peter said without any controversy or misunderstanding.

[18] *Forasmuch as ye know that ye were not redeemed with corruptible things, as silver and gold, from your vain conversation received by tradition from your fathers;*
[19] *But with the precious blood of Christ, as of a lamb without blemish and without spot:*

[23] Being born again, not of corruptible seed, but of incorruptible, by the word of God, which lives and abides forever   I Peter 1: 18-19, 23

The Apostle Paul wrote.
But we are bound to give thanks always to God for you, brethren beloved of the Lord, because God hath from the beginning chosen you to salvation through sanctification of the Spirit and belief of the truth
II Thessalonians 2:13

Note the two ingredients that are necessary for a person to be saved or born again: (1) The work of the Spirit and the (2) Presence of the Word of God. One must have the Spirit at work in his heart, must believe the Word of Truth. One cannot hear and believe the Holy Bible without the Holy Spirit to lead you and guide you. . One cannot be sanctified by the Spirit (Holy Spirit) unless one receives the guarantee and seal of the Holy Spirit…..YOU MUST BE BORN AGAIN.

Christianity affirms the presence and role of the Holy Ghost in the *The Apostles Creed*, which identifies one, united body of Christians called the *Holy Catholic Church*. The word *catholic* does not mean the Roman Catholic Church, but was meant to mean the *universal church* or the *body of Christ*, and these were the words used in the original version of the Creed. The Apostles creed is regularly read in many different Christian denominations today. The phrase, *He descended into hell,* was later added and was not a part of the creed in its earliest form. This phrase is usually identified with I Peter 3:18-19 and Acts 2:31, and seems to have been added by *Rufinus* in the

THE APOSTLES CREED

I BELIEVE IN GOD THE FATHER ALMIGHTY, MAKER OF HEAVEN AND EARTH, AND IN JESUS CHRIST HIS ONLY SON OUR LORD, WHO WAS CONCEIVED BY THE HOLY GHOST, BORN OF THE VIRGIN MARY, SUFFERED UNDER PONTIUS PILATE, WAS CRUCIFIED, DEAD, AND BURIED. HE DESCENDED INTO HELL; THE THIRD DAY HE ROSE AGAIN FROM THE DEAD; HE ASCENDED INTO HEAVEN, AND SITTETH ON THE RIGHT HAND OF GOD THE FATHER ALMIGHTY; FROM THENCE HE SHALL COME TO JUDGE THE QUICK AND THE DEAD. I BELIEVE IN THE HOLY GHOST; THE HOLY CATHOLIC CHURCH, THE COMMUNION OF SAINTS; THE FORGIVENESS OF SINS; THE RESURRECTION OF THE BODY, AND THE LIFE EVERLASTING.
AMEN.

late fourth century AD, and was not officially adopted into the original creed until about 650 AD.

The Holy Spirit and the role which it plays in a New Covenant Christian is a topic which needs to be taught more often in churches today.

A Christian should not feel uncomfortable accepting that the Holy Spirit is a part of their social and religious life. The multiple gifts which God imparts to everyone who is born again enables each Christian to be more effective when teaching and preaching the Gospel message. Orthodox Christianity has affirmed since the earliest days of church history that the Holy Spirit and the Son are both one with the Father, and both always agree with the thoughts and actions of the sovereign Father. Jesus Christ affirmed that *He never spoke or did anything unless the Father told Him to do so* (John 5:19, John 12:49). In the same manner, the Holy Spirit acts and speaks to our own spirit and will tell us only what God has revealed to Him (I John 5: 7-8, Galatians 4:6)

The Bible declares that the Holy Spirit is *the power of God* (2 Timothy 1:7); it *leads us into all truth* (John 14:17, 26); He enables us to *discern spiritual things* (1 Corinthians 2:11, 14), He is our *guarantee* (seal) of our *salvation* (Ephesians 1: 13-14). *Without* the Holy Spirit that dwells within us, we are *not His* (Romans 8:9. The average Christian is casually aware of how the Holy Spirit is present in every born-again believer, but fails to understand the real power which is given to us by the Holy Spirit.

The Holy Spirit brings 9 special gifts when it comes to dwell in every Born-again Christian. These will be discussed in Chapter 3. The Holy Spirit can be characterized and explained by examining six different categories.

  (1) *Manifestation* of the Holy Spirit
  (2) *Baptism* of the Holy Spirit

(3) *Role* of the Holy Spirit
(4) *Purpose* of the Holy Spirit in every believer
(5) *Presence* of the Holy Spirit in every born-again Christian
(6) *Power* of the Holy Spirit.

Manifestation of the Holy Spirit

The Holy Spirit cannot be found in every person. It is a gift that is given to every Christian who is *born again*. The Holy Scriptures declare that the Holy Spirit is *the power of God* (2 Timothy 1:7); it *leads us to all truth* (John 14:17, 26); it enables us to *discern spiritual things* (I Corinthians 2:11, 14); it is our *guarantee (seal) of eternal life* (Ephesians 1:13-14), and *without* it we are *not His* (Romans 8:9).

Perhaps the most important thing that the Holy Spirit does for every born-again Christian is to baptize that believer into Jesus Christ. The baptism by the Holy Spirit can be defined as that work whereby the Spirit of God places the believer into union with Christ and into a joining together with other believers in the body of Christ This is a spiritual transformation by which every true believer becomes a part of the body of Christ. As a member of the body of Christ, one becomes an heir and joint heir to all of the promises.

The Phrase *born again* is first used by Christ in John Chapter 3. A ruler of the Jews called Nicodemus had evidently heard the gospel message, received it, and wanted to be saved. He came to Jesus by night and spoke:

Rabbi, we know that thou art a teacher come from God: for no man can do these miracles that thou doest, except God be with him   John 3:2

Jesus Christ, knowing the true thoughts and heart of all men, perceived that the man wanted to accept Him as the Son of God and his redeemer. He responded to Nicodemus with a strange command.

Verily, verily, I say unto thee: Except a man be born again, he cannot see the kingdom of God   John 3:3

This must have startled and confused Nicodemus because he then asked:

How can a man be born when he is old? can he enter the second time into his mother's womb, and be born?   John 3:4

Jesus told Nicodemus:

[6] *That which is born of the flesh is flesh; and that which is born of the Spirit is spirit.*
[7] *Marvel not that I said unto thee,* **Ye must be born again**.
[8] *The wind blows where it will, and you hear the sound, but cannot tell whence it cometh, and whither it goeth: so is every one that is born of the Spirit.*
[9] *Nicodemus answered and said unto him, How can these things be?*
[10] *Jesus answered and said unto him, Art thou a master of Israel, and knowest not these things?*   John 3: 8-10

Jesus rebukes Nicodemus and tells him that: *You are a ruler of the Jews and do not know these things?* Nicodemus had previously asked; *How can these things be?* Jesus had already revealed the meaning of His direct response.

[12] *But as many as received him, to them he gave power to become the sons of God, even to them that believe on his name:*
[13] *Which were born, not of blood, nor of the will of the flesh, nor of the will of man, but of God.*   John 1: 12-13

The phrase *born again* means to be reborn spiritually. Nicodemus needed a change in his heart…... a spiritual transformation. …… birth into a new creature who would be conformed to the image and will of Jesus Christ; not his own. Being born again, is an act of God which takes place at the moment anyone chooses to believe and follow the commands of Jesus Christ. Salvation is imparted to the person who believes (2 Corinthians 5:17; Titus 3:5; 1 Peter 1:3; 1 John 2:29; 3:9; 4:7; 5:1-4, 18). John 1:12, 13). Being born again also involves becoming a son of God by trusting in the name of Jesus Christ. *How does this transformation take place?*

The agent by which a person is born again is by the *Holy Spirit.* Once a person believes and accepts Jesus Christ as their Lord and Savior, they immediately receive the gift of the Holy Spirit from Jesus Christ. It is by and through the Holy Spirit that a person is *baptized into the body of Christ*.

Baptism of the Holy Spirit
The apostle John said:

Baptism of the Holy Spirit

I knew him not: but he that sent me to baptize with water, the same said unto me: Upon whom thou shalt see the Spirit descending, and remaining on him, the same is he which baptizes with the Holy Ghost.   John 1:33

Paul explained this when he revealed the *mystery* of the New Covenant. *For by one Spirit are we all baptized into one body, whether we be Jews or Gentiles, whether we be bond or free; and have been all made to drink into one Spirit*   I Corinthians 12:13

For as many of you as have been baptized into Christ have put on Christ Galatians 3:27

For John truly baptized with water; but ye shall be baptized with the Holy Ghost not many days hence   Acts 1:5

Know ye not, that so many of us as were baptized into Jesus Christ were baptized into his death?   Romans 6:3

> Baptism of the Holy Spirit can be defined as that work whereby the Spirit of God places the believer into union with Christ, and into a common spiritual body with other believers at the moment of salvation. The baptism of the Holy Spirit was predicted by John the Baptist (Mark 1:8) and by Jesus before He ascended to heaven: *For John baptized with water, but in a few days you will be baptized with the Holy Spirit* (Acts 1:5).
>
> This promise was fulfilled on the Day of Pentecost (Acts 2: 1–4) where for the first time, people were permanently indwelt by the Holy Spirit. Being in the *body of Christ* means that we are risen with Him to newness of life (Romans 6:4). We should then exercise our spiritual gifts to keep the body of Christ functioning properly.   Taken from *Got questions.org*

After the Jews were baptized with the Holy Ghost on the Day of Pentecost, salvation and forgiveness of sin was rejected by the Jewish Spiritual leaders. When the Jews turned away from Jesus Christ, God turned to the Gentiles. He chose Paul to announce the mystery of the New Covenant, and the Holy spirit was sent to every Jew and Gentile who would believe upon our Lord and Savior Jesus Christ.

Personification of The Holy Spirit

The Holy Bible in the New Testament has much to say about the personification of the Holy Spirit in every Born-again believer's life. Any Christian will recognize the rightful place of the Holy Spirit as a member of the eternal triad of God the Father,

Jesus Christ the Son and the Holy Spirit, but few can speak of the manifold presentation and

[7] But the manifestation of the Spirit is given to every man to profit withal.
[8] For to one is given by the Spirit the word of wisdom; to another the word of knowledge by the same Spirit;
[9] To another faith by the same Spirit; to another the gifts of healing by the same Spirit;
[10] To another the working of miracles; to another prophecy; to another discerning of spirits; to another different kinds of tongues; to another the interpretation of tongues:
[11] **But all these worketh that one and the selfsame Spirit,** *dividing to every man severally as he will   I Corinthians 12: 7-11*

The first thing that happens to any individual who has been spiritually born-again is that he/she becomes a new creature in Jesus Christ. The old passes away, and all things are made new in Jesus Christ. That person becomes a part of Jesus Christ and is heir to all of the promises. This is called a *baptism* by the Holy Spirit. The Holy Spirit baptizes a new Born-again Christian into Christ. The set of all believers is called the *body of Christ*.

Now ye are the **body of Christ***, and members in particular*
I Corinthians 12:27

Once a Born-again Christian becomes a new creature in Christ, the Holy Spirit is sent to dwell in that individual. The Holy Spirit then activates different Gifts of the Holy Spirit as God directs Him to do so. Particular gifts are granted to each individual to carry out the work of the ministry. The power to use these gifts is also through the Holy Spirit. This new life in Christ manifests itself through service, and that individual is rewarded the *Fruits of the Spirit*.

The Holy Spirit is the spiritual force by which every true Christian is *sealed* and *baptized* into the Body of Christ. When every Christian is Born-again, The Holy Spirit is given and resides in that person. We need to fully understand why the Holy Spirit is given. The Holy Spirit under the New Covenant has:

        (1) *Purpose*

              (2) *Prescence* and

                      (3) *Power*.

Purpose of the Holy Spirit

The Holy Spirit occupies a pivotal role as each Christian attempts to understand God., As a third person of the Holy Trinity, the Holy Spirit is unique because He comes to reside in each Born Again Christian., Jesus Christ said: *When the Spirit of Truth comes, he will guide you into all truth* (John 16:13. The Word of Truth contains the instructions for discerning and following God's will, and understanding of that truth is imparted to all believers by the Holy Spirit.

Purpose of the Holy Spirit

The Holy Spirit also serves as a *comforter* and *advocate* (John 14:16), facilitating a personal relationship between God and believers. *The Spirit himself testifies with our spirit that we are God's children* (Romans 8:16).

The transformative work of the Holy Spirit includes *sanctification*; the process by which believers are made holy through their union with Christ (2 Thessalonians 2:13). In this context, the Holy Spirit is responsible for allocating spiritual gifts to all Born-again believers. (Galatians 5:22-23), The fruits of spiritual gifts manifest themselves through the Holy Spirit as love, joy, peace, and other qualities that reflect Christ's character.

This emphasizes the Holy Spirit's function as a source of empowerment, enabling each believer to contribute uniquely to the communal life of the Church and to the advancement of the Gospel. Through these gifts, the Holy Spirit fosters diversity within unity, illustrating how individual talents and abilities can be harmonized for a common purpose and mission. The *Gifts of the Holy Spirit* to each Born-again Christian cannot be discerned, they are given to each individual to carry out the work of the ministry. What can be readily discerned are the Fruits of the Holy Spirit.

Presence of the Holy Spirit

Presence of the Holy Spirit

The presence of the Holy Spirit plays a crucial role in the process of regeneration and spiritual rebirth, marking the spiritual beginning of a believer's Born-again-walk with Christ. In Titus 3:5, the Spirit is described as the agent who brings about cleansing and renewal of true believers. This mission of the depth of the Spirit's work is not merely as a passive presence, but as an active force that initiates spiritual awakening and guides believers toward righteousness. Through regeneration, the believer receives a new identity in Jesus Christ and becomes a member of the family of God. The Holy spirit is continually active in building up and sustaining the faith of every believer. Hence, the Holy Spirit's dynamic role encompasses empowerment, gifting, transformation, and new life… reflecting the love and sustaining power of the Father.

When Christ spoke to His apostles just before He was arrested and crucified, he told them the following:

[7] *Nevertheless I tell you the truth; It is expedient for you that I go away: for if I go not away, the Comforter will not come unto you; but if I depart, I will send him unto you.*

[8] And when he is come, he will reprove the world of sin, and of righteousness, and of judgment:
[9] Of sin, because they believe not on me;
[10] Of righteousness, because I go to my Father, and ye see me no more;
[11] Of judgment, because the prince of this world is judged.
[12] I have yet many things to say unto you, but ye cannot bear them now.
[13] Howbeit when he, the Spirit of truth, is come, he will guide you into all truth: for he shall not speak of himself; but whatsoever he shall hear, that shall he speak: and he will shew you things to come.
[14] He shall glorify me: for he shall receive of mine, and shall shew it unto you   John 16: 7-14

Jesus Christ promised His disciples that He would not leave them helpless, but that after He is gone, He would send them the great *comforter*, which is another term for the *Holy Spirit*. This first happened on the Day of Pentecost, when the Holy Spirit fell upon each apostle and 3000 other Jews who had gathered in Jerusalem. After salvation was offered first to the Jews on the day of Pentecost, the Jewish religious leaders rejected Jesus Christ as their Messiah and persecuted new Jewish converts. After the Jews stoned Steven, Jesus turned to the Gentiles and anointed Paul to reveal the *mystery* of the New Covenant.

As a part of the New Covenant, the Holy Spirit is promised to everyone who becomes a born-again Christian. There are several specific spiritual transformations which take place when each individual gives their life to Jesus Christ.

- The word is *received*
- The word is *believed.*
- That person is *Born-again* and receives the *Holy Spirit*
- Any person that truly believes and gives their life to Jesus Christ is a *New Creature* in Jesus Christ.

The apostle Paul wrote:

So, then faith cometh by hearing, and hearing by the word of God
Romans 10:17

When every word that is written in the Word of Truth is *received* and then *believed*, the Holy Spirit will begin to transform that person into a *New Creature* that has been Born-again into the likeness of Jesus Christ.

Therefore, if any man be in Christ, he is a new creature: old things are passed away; behold, all things are become new   II Corinthians 5:17

Power of the Holy Spirit

One of the prominent roles of the Holy Spirit in each believer is to give the gift of *power*. Like every other gift, power is sent by God through the Holy Spirit. Spiritual power is very important to the ministry of Jesus Christ, and the advancement of His Kingdom. The last thing that Christ told His apostles and disciples was that He would send them the gift of *power* to accomplish His goals.

Power of the Holy Spirit

But ye shall receive power, after that the Holy Ghost is come upon you: and ye shall be witnesses unto me both in Jerusalem, and in all Judaea, and in Samaria, and unto the uttermost part of the earth   Acts 1:8

What exactly did Christ mean when He promised power? The Kingdom of God and the transformation of sinful man to conform to the nature of Christ is a supernatural transformation. It is not physical but spiritual, and the concept of power as defined by man cannot accomplish such a transformation. During His earthly ministry, Jesus said that He possessed all power in heaven and on earth.

And Jesus came and spoke unto them, saying: All power is given unto me in heaven and in earth   Matthew 28:18

Jesus returned from His 40 days in the wilderness in the *power* of the Holy Spirit (Luke 4:14). Jesus stated publicly that all *power* in heaven and in earth had been given to Him (Matthew 28:18).
This same power was made manifest to all of His disciples (Luke 9:1). The gift of *power* equips us to do His work and spread the gospel. One of the prerequisites to receive Holy Spirit power is to live by *faith*.

Without faith, it is impossible to please God   Hebrews 11:6

[16] This I say then: Walk in the Spirit, and ye shall not fulfill the lust of the flesh.
[17] For the flesh lusts against the Spirit, and the Spirit against the flesh: and these are contrary the one to the other: so that ye cannot do the things that ye would   Galatians 5: 16-17

*Pow*e*r* provides a true believer:

- The *capability* to speak boldly with authority
- The *wisdom* to speak and teach effectively
- The *ability* to change the behavior of others.

These are all power gifts from God to carry out the Ministry of Christ in His absence… Because the power of the Holy Spirit is literally the power of God, the ability to act and influence is infinite, unlimited, and eternal. In this way, the power of the Holy Spirit is different from any other kind of power. All the manifold power of God belongs to the children of God as their birthright in Christ. The Holy Spirit allocates, develops, and sustains spiritual gifts in every true believer to conduct Spiritual warfare and win souls to Christ. By His power and authority to conduct warfare against evil and sin, all believers should never fear Satan. The Holy Spirit permanently resides in everyone who has been Born-again, and imparts two things to every true believer:

(1) *Gifts* of the Holy Spirit
(2) *Fruits* of the Holy Spirit

Matthew 7:16-18

"By their fruit you will recognize them. Do people pick grapes from thornbushes, or figs from thistles? Likewise, every good tree bears good fruit, but a bad tree bears bad fruit. A good tree cannot bear bad fruit, and a bad tree cannot bear good fruit."

Gifts of the Holy Spirit

The Holy Spirit is a multi-faceted, spiritual being who brings unique skills and abilities to individuals in both the Old and New Testaments. The Gifts of the Spirit come from God through the Holy Spirit (Called Spirit of God in Old Testament). The Gifts of the Spirit are different in the Old Testament and in the New Testament. They represent a special set of skills and abilities by which God empowers men and women to do what He has called us to do.

According as his divine power hath given unto us all things that pertain unto life and godliness, through the knowledge of him that hath called us to glory and virtue   II Peter 1:3

The gifts of the Holy Spirit provide *everything that is needed* to accomplish what God has predestined for your life in Christ. It is seldom recognized, but these gifts are different in number and type between the Old and New Testaments.

The gifts of the Holy Spirit are given in Isaiah 11:2.
 in the Old Testament.

[1] *And there shall come forth a rod out of the stem of Jesse, and a Branch shall grow out of his roots:*
[2] *And the Spirit of the LORD shall rest upon him, the spirit of **wisdom** and **understanding**, the spirit of **counsel** and **might**, the spirit of **knowledge** and of the **fear of the LORD***
Isaiah 11: 1-2

The Isaiah prophecy is Messianic, list only 6 gifts: (1) Wisdom (2) Understanding, (3) Counsel (4) Might (5) Knowledge and (6) Fear of the Lord. The Roman Catholic church added a 7th added a seventh gift; *piety*. This was done to achieve the symbolic number for completeness, which is the number *seven*. The 7th gift is by Catholic edict, and should not be included. These 7 gifts will be discused in Chapter 2.

Jesus was blessed with all of these gifts by his Father, and those who are Born-again are blessed with these gifts by the Holy Spirit. The Holy Spirit supplies the spiritual power and strength a person needs to accomplish his or her calling in Jesus Christ. Each of these 6 gifts will be discussed in Chapter 2. The Holy Spirt operates within any Born-again Christian in the New Covenant in a different way than in the Old Covenant. The apostle Paul spoke of different *gifts* which are given to a true Christian when they receive Christ as their Lord and Savior. Luke listed 9 gifts in the Book of Acts, and Paul again listed them in I Corinthians 12: 7-11.

These 9 gifts are *available* to every true believer, but they are not all *activated* in each Born-again believer. These 9 gifts are manifested by the Holy Spirit, but they all come from God Almighty.

They come from God and reside in every Born-again believer along with the Holy Spirit when they accept Jesus Christ as Lord and Savior. Each of these 9 gifts will be discussed in Chapter 3.

The *Fruits* of The Holy Spirit
The Fruits of the Holy Spirit can only be found in a complete, Spirit-filled Christian. They are listed by Paul in Galatians 5: 22-23: (1) Love (2) Joy (3) Peace (4) Longsuffering (5) Gentleness (6) Goodness (7) Faith (8) Meekness and (9)

Temperance. Just think what the world would be like if everyone loved his neighbor as himself and lived under the credo of these 9 gifts. The world of unbelievers seeks to find these 9 gifts, but they cannot be found. Only a Christian who is sure that he/she will be saved from their sins by Jesus Christ and is assured of eternal life can ever achieve a state of existence which God by the *fruits of the Spirit* blesses that individual for service. One who can go through life joined to Jesus Christ can truly find the *Kingdom of Heaven* here on earth. These things are what will be found in God's eternal Kingdom. This what Matthew meant when he declared:

From that time Jesus began to preach, and to say: Repent: for the **Kingdom of Heaven** *is at hand*   Matthew 4:17

We are to place all our cares, our woes, and our sorrows upon Him. He wants us to come to Him as little children and believe that only He is *the way, the truth, and the life* (John 14:6). Who would want to live any other way?

[16] *This I say then, Walk in the Spirit, and ye shall not fulfill the lust of the flesh.*
[17] *For the flesh lusts against the Spirit, and the Spirit against the flesh: and these are contrary the one to the other: so that ye cannot do the things that ye would.*
[18] *But if ye be led of the Spirit, ye are not under the law.*
[19] *Now the works of the flesh are manifest, which are these; Adultery, fornication, uncleanness, lasciviousness,*

[20] Idolatry, witchcraft, hatred, variance, emulations, wrath, strife, seditions, heresies,
[21] Enviers, murders, drunkenness, retellings, and such like: of the which I tell you before, as I have also told you in time past, that they which do such things shall not inherit the kingdom of God.
[22] But the fruit of the Spirit is love, joy, peace, longsuffering, gentleness, goodness, faith,
[23] Meekness, temperance: against such there is no law.
[24] And they that are Christ's have crucified the flesh with the affections and lusts.
[25] If we live in the Spirit, let us also walk in the Spirit
Galatians 5: 16-25

*What? know ye not that your **body** is the temple of the Holy Ghost which is in you, which ye have of God, and ye are not your own?*
I Corinthians 6:19

This is another *mystery* which is difficult to comprehend. God the Father, God the Son, and God the Holy spirit…...A triune Godhead which is of one mind, one accord and one in agreement of all things. The Holy Spirit has been sent by God at the request of Jesus Christ to dwell inside of every true believer (John 14:6, John 14:16). This is a true and uncomprehensible *mystery* which is not explained in the Holy Scriptures.

The average Christian does not fully understand or recognize the power which resides in the Holy Spirit. *Each Christian* is given a gift of the Holy Spirit when they turn to him as their Lord and Savior and are Born-again. The Holy Spirit baptizes each born-again Christian into the body of Jesus Christ, and then bestows upon each individual gifts from on high, by which every Christian can function in a world of sin and unrighteousness. When a Christian lives in Christ and uses the gifts which the Holy Spirit gives, the result is Joy, love and peace which passes all understanding… these are the fruits of the Holy Spirit. This is the power that we can be given and victory that we have in Jesus Christ.

It is almost universally recognized that the Holy spirit has been active in God's plan for mankind, but when pressed to give examples of the work of the Holy Spirit in both the Old and New Testaments, most modern Christians will not be able to do so. Chapter 2 will discuss how the Holy Spirit was active in the Old Testament, and Chapter 3 will explore the importance of the Holy Spirit in the New Covenant.

Chapter 2
The Holy Spirit in the Old Testament

In the both the Old and New Testaments, it is rare to find the term *Holy Spirit*. The term *Holy Spirit* is casually used by theologians, but it is only used three times in two verses in the Old Testament (Psalms 51:11 and Isaiah 63:11). The Apostle Paul and Luke are the only New Testament writers who uses this term (Ephesians 1:13, Ephesians 4:30, I Thessalonians 4:8, Luke 11:13). The most common identifier is the *Spirit of God* (19 times in the Old Testament and 15 times in the New Testament) or simply the *Spirit*. The Hebrew word for *spirit* is *ruah* or *ruach*. It appears 389 times in the Old Testament in a wide context. It is used to identify an attribute and a characteristic of God (136 times).

The most basic meaning of *ruach* is *wind* (113 times). *Ruah* swept over the waters (Genesis 1:2); and the Lord walked in the garden in the wind (Genesis 3:8). A wind (ruah) brought locusts upon Egypt as the 8th plague (Exodus 10:13)) and a strong east wind divided the Red Sea during the Exodus (Exodus 14:21). A frequent use of *ruach* is *Breath*. It is the Lord who gives breath to all people (Isaiah 42:5), and to lifeless bodies (Ezekial 37: 9-10). In the New Testament, the equivalent Greek word for *ruach* is *pneuma*, which has been translated as both *wind and spirit* (John 3:5, John 3:8).

When the Holy Spirit is either used or implied, it is always in masculine form. The translators from Greek and Latin into English decided to capitalize "Spirit" when it came from God, and used lower case "spirit" when it was not of divine origin. The Holy Spirit is usually called the *Spirit of the Lord*, the *Spirit of God* or just the *Spirit*. Proceeding with caution, we will treat these three terms as the Holy Spirit. Depending upon context, The Holy Spirit is also associated with the third person of the Holy Trinity (Father-Son-Holy Spirit). The first occurrence of the Holy Spirit seems to be in Genesis 1:2 when the world was created where the Holy Spirit was called the *Spirit of God*.

*And the earth was without form, and void; and darkness was upon the face of the deep. And the **Spirit of God** moved upon the face of the waters.* Genesis 1:2

Genesis 1 seems to indicate that the Holy Spirit was not the *agent* of creation (God was), but He certainly was *active* when the world was created and had some role in the creative process.

As we try to find actions in the Old Testament in which the Holy Spirit is involved, it seems that the Spirit is given to selected people to execute the will of God…particularly to defeat the enemies of Israel. Gideon (Judges 6:34), Sampson in Judges 5:14, and King David (I Samuel 16:13) were all anointed with the Holy Spirit. The prophet Joel implies that the Spirit of God in the Old Testament is the same as the Holy Spirit in the New Testament, when he prophesied of the Holy Spirit falling upon redeemed Jews on the Day of Pentecost (Joel 2).

[28] And it shall come to pass afterward, that I will pour out my Spirit upon all flesh; and your sons and your daughters shall prophesy, your old men shall dream dreams, your young men shall see visions:
[29] And also upon the servants and upon the handmaids in those days will I pour out my Spirit Joel 2: 28-29

Genesis 6:3 suggests that the Holy Spirit in the Old Testament was given to prophets to boldly rebuke sin. The prophet Micah condemned the house of Jacob and the nation of Israel for their sins against God. Micah admonished evil and declared the righteousness of God, and he attributed his boldness to the Spirit of the Lord (Micah 3:8). Micah said the Spirit filled him with *justice and might.*

Isaiah prophesied about Israel's coming Messiah, noting that the Spirit would rest upon Him (Isaiah 42:1). The Holy Spirit was a powerful presence from the time of creation and throughout the history of Israel, right up to the coming of Jesus Christ.

The widespread use of the term Holy Spirit by both theologians and Christians is undoubtedly due to the belief in a Holy Trinity, consisting of the Father, Son, and the Holy Spirit. The Holy Trinity has been the subject of theological discussion for over 1500 years, and has been violently defended and defined by multiple denominations in different ways. The term Holy Trinity is man-made, and cannot be found in the Holy Scriptures. It is inferred from the full council of scriptures. The Father, Son and Holy Ghost is only used once in all of the King James Bible (Matthew 28:19).

The Greek word *pneuma* is commonly found in the King James translation of the Holy Bible. It is translated as "**S**pirit" 138 times and as "**s**pirit" 123 times. The New International Version translates pneuma as "**S**pirit" 246 times and as "**s**pirit" 92 times. This is quite a difference…. Why? The King James version of English translated from the Greek language used spirit, Spirit and Holy Spirit, but with little justification. This is usually ignored. However, it is suggested that the correct translation and usage is important, particularly in the 13 epistles of Paul. In general, the Holy Spirit (caps) is used to identify the 3rd member of the triune Godhead (Father, Son, and Holy Spirit). The Holy Spirit is sent from God at the request of His Son Jesus Christ, and is called the

Spirit of Truth in John 15:26. Note that Jesus Christ is said to *proceed* from God the Father in John 8:42. In some mysterious way, God will send the Holy Spirit from His Spirit to dwell in *every* born-again believer. This will be discussed again in Chapter 3, but for now note that this identifies the Holy Spirit as being part of God the Father, and this is why it should be capitalized.

> *Authors Note*: In the Authorized King James Version of the Bible, the translators capitalized *God* wherever it referred to God the Father. There are many secular "gods", and when the word "**g**od" is used to denote a heathen god, it is lower case. Similarly, man was created by **G**od (upper case). When referring to the *spirit* of man it should always be lower case. The 3rd use of *pneuma* and the Greek word *paraclete* is to refer to a function of the Holy Spirit. Paraclete is a Christian biblical term occurring five times in the Johannine texts of the New Testament. In Christian theology, the word commonly refers to the Holy Spirit and is translated as *advocate, counsellor*, or *helper*. To resolve this apparent conflict and remain true to the original meanings, this book will capitalize all translated words which refer to God the Father and use caps (e.g.… Holy Spirit). All other translations of *paraclete* or *ruach* will use lower case. A careful study of these terms is beyond the scope of this book, but it is one worthy of time spent.

As previously discussed, the term Holy Spirit is only used 3 times in two verses of the Old Testament. The *Holy Spirit* is designated as either the *Spirit of God*, or the *Spirit of the Lord* 124 times. The role of the Holy Spirit in the Old Testament was not as extensive in the New Testament.

However, the Holy Spirit was very active. There are 10 major areas in which the Holy Spirit was involved in the Old Testament.

1.0 *The Holy Spirit was active in the Creation Process*

The Holy Spirit played an active role when God created the heavens and the earth (Genesis 1:2). Only God had the power to create the heavens and the earth, but the Holy Spirit and The Word (Jesus Christ, John 1:1) was directly involved in the creative process. It is difficult if not impossible to arrive at any firm conclusion about the exact nature and extent of their work, but we know that the Holy Spirit (Spirit of God) moved upon the *face of the waters.* Note that this was before the earth was divided into firmament and oceans. It was without form and in the Greek (*Tohu*) it was *empty*. The Holy Spirit was *moving* (*rachaph*) over the waters (Genesis 1:2). Evidently, the earth had water upon its face but without any sea or fresh water creatures. These were not created until the 5th day. The Holy Spirit was also involved in initiating the birth cycles of all living creatures (Psalms 104:30).

2.0 *The Holy Spirit was Sent by God to Accomplish Specific Things in His divine Plan for Mankind*

In the Old Testament God anointed certain individuals to carry out His divine will. The following examples will demonstrate how God gave the Holy Spirit to certain people.

3.0 *Bezalel was chosen by God to build the Tabernacle.*

He was given supernatural skills to construct the Tabernacle according to the specific plans given to Moses by God.

[1] *And the LORD spoke unto Moses, saying,*
[2] *See, I have called by name Bezaleel the son of Uri, the son of Hur, of the tribe of Judah:*
[3] *And I have filled him with the spirit of God, in wisdom,*

and in understanding, and in knowledge, and in all manner of workmanship   Exodus 1:1-3

4.0   The Lord Anointed Moses and the 70 Elders

[16] And the LORD said unto Moses, Gather unto me seventy men of the elders of Israel, whom thou knowest to be the elders of the people, and officers over them; and bring them unto the tabernacle of the congregation, that they may stand there with thee.

*[17] And I will come down and talk with thee there: and **I will take of the spirit which is upon thee, and will put it upon them**; and they shall bear the burden of the people with thee, that thou bear it not thyself alone*   Numbers 11: 16-17

Note something unique about this Old Testament anointing. This is the first time that God anointed a group of people all at once, and it is was not directly but the Spirit of God came from Moses

5.0   The Lord anointed Joshua to assume the leadership of Israel when he replaced Moses as Commander-in-Chief.

And Joshua the son of Nun was full of the spirit of wisdom; for Moses had laid his hands upon him: and the children of Israel hearkened unto him, and did as the LORD commanded Moses   Joshua 34:9

Note that Joshua was filled with the *wisdom* of the Holy Spirit.

6.0   Saul was Anointed with the Spirit of God

When God rescued the Israelites from Egyptian slavery, the form of government was an absolute *Monarchy*. He alone was the supreme and sovereign King of Israel. God ruled according to a set of commands and laws that could not be violated. As time passed, Israel wanted to have a physical King just like every other nation, and so they pleaded with God and Samuel to give them a King as other nations. Reluctantly, knowing the eventual outcome, God acquiesced and allowed Saul to be chosen as the 1st King of Israel. When the people chose Saul, God gave him the Holy spirit to rule and reign wisely.

7.0 King David was Anointed with the Holy Spirit

Then Samuel took the horn of oil, and anointed him in the midst of his brethren: and the Spirit of the LORD came upon David from that day forward   I Samuel 16:13

There is a debate among Christians and theologians as to whether the Holy Spirit can be removed from a person or whether it can never be lost. This narrative seems to fully answer this question, but perhaps only in the Old Testament. Note also that King David received the Spirit of God when he became King after Saul died, but David was concerned that the Lord might remove the Spirit from him after He had sinned.

*Cast me not away from thy presence; and take not thy **Holy Spirit** from me*   Psalms 51:11

> The Spirit of God in the Old Testament was placed inside certain individuals to accomplish specific tasks or assignments. In the Old Testament, the Spirit was also removed by God for disobedience and sinful behavior. We will address whether the Holy Spirit can be removed by God during the New Testament in Chapter 5.

8.0 Sampson was Anointed

[5] *Then went Samson down, and his father and his mother, to Timnath, and came to the vineyards of Timnath: and, behold, a young lion roared against him*

[6] And the Spirit of the LORD came mightily upon him, and he rent him as he would have rent a kid, and he had nothing in his hand: but he told not his father or his mother what he had done   Judges 4: 5-6

Sampson was one of the great heroes of the Old Testament. In the Book of Judges, we read that Samson was able to accomplish great things because the *Spirit of the Lord* came upon him… at least 5 times (Judges 13:25, Judges 14: Judges 5-9, Judges 14:19, Judges 15:14). He took the Nazarite vow and committed himself to serving a life for God (Judges 13: 4-5, Numbers 6: 1-8). Samson insisted on doing things his way. He began by ignoring God's prohibition about marrying someone outside his faith. Samson also violated his Nazarite vow by touching the dead (Judges 14: 8-9) and drinking wine (Judges 14:10). Part of his Nazarite Vow was to never cut his hair (Numbers 6:5). The Spirit of the Lord was upon Samson, but He thought that he was invincible because of his great strength. Sampson was conquered not by a superior opponent, but by a Philistine woman named Delilah who cut off his hair with a razor (Judges 16: 17-29). How are we to understand the fall of Sampson? Samson ignored the voice of God, and did whatever he pleased: And he violated his Nazarite vow. When he lost his strength and his anointing, he turned back to God who allowed Sampson to destroy a Philistine temple and die with everyone there. Sampson had the full anointing of the Spirit of God, but he lost it… regained it…and redeemed his sinful ways. His problem was the middle verb in *sin…. I*.

In addition to those individuals previously discussed, the following people were anointed for specific tasks in the Old Testament.

- **Bezalel** was *filled* with the *Spirit of God* to develop and execute artistic design for the Tabernacle (Exodus 31:2; Exodus 35:31)

- **Balaam** temporarily received the Spirit of God when he saw that it pleased God for him to bless Israel (Numbers 24: 1-6)
- **Joshua** was given the Holy spirit when he replaced Moses to enter the Land of Canaan (Numbers 27:18)
- **Othniel** was given the Spirit of the Lord when he was chosen to war against Chushan-Rishathaim, king of Mesopotamia (Judges 3:9-10)
- **Japheth** was given the Spirit of the Lord when the Ammonites refused Israel to pass through their land, and Japheth defeated them in battle (Judges 11: 28-33)
- **Isaiah** received the Spirit of God when he prophesied of a man (Jesus Christ) who would be sent by God to redeem Israel (Isaiah 59:21)
- **Ezekiel** was given the *Spirit* when God chose him to speak to Israel concerning their sinful and rebellious nature. Later God visited him again with an anointing by the *Spirit* when God told him to warn Israel of persecutions and oppression which would come upon them (Ezekiel 2: 1-3, Ezekiel 3:24)
- The Spirit of God came upon **Amasai** as he spoke to the tribes of the Northern Kingdom (I Chronicles 12:18)
- **Jahaziel** the son of Zachariah was anointed with the Spirit of God as he spoke to King David and the Kingdom of Judah concerning whether Judah should go to war against Moab and Ammon (II Chronicles 20 14)
- **Prophets** of old spoke when the Spirit of God gave them utterance (II Chronicles 15:1, II Chronicles 20:14, II Chronicles 24:20, Joel 2:28-29)

Gifts of the Holy Spirit in Old Testament

Isaiah identified gifts of the Holy Spirit which can only come from God. They were delivered to man by the Spirit of the Lord in the Old Testament.

[1] *And there shall come forth a rod out of the stem of Jesse, and a Branch shall grow out of his roots:*
[2] *And the Spirit of the LORD shall rest upon him, the Spirit of **wisdom** and **understanding**, the Spirit of **counsel** and **might**, the Spirit of **knowledge** and of the **fear of the LORD***
Isaiah 11: 1-2

The Isaiah prophecy identifies the Spirit of the Lord (Holy Spirit) as the agent of delivery. The *Spirit of the Lord* in the *Old Testament* is the same as the *Holy Spirit* in the *New Testament*. Isaiah actually identified only 6 gifts. The Roman Catholic Church later added a seventh gift which they called *piety*. This was done to achieve the symbolic number for completeness, which is the number **seven**.

These 6 gifts were not available to every Jew in the Old Testament. They were sent by God to accomplish specific tasks, or they were sent to Kings to reign wisely. Proper use of these gifts requires dedication, maturity, and *Fear of the Lord*.

The 6 gifts of the Holy Spirit identified by Isaiah are an antitype of the Holy Menorah type which stood in the Holy Place of the Tabernacle. There was one central pipe which provided *oil* (Holy Spirit) to each of the 7 branches (Gifts of Holy Spirit).

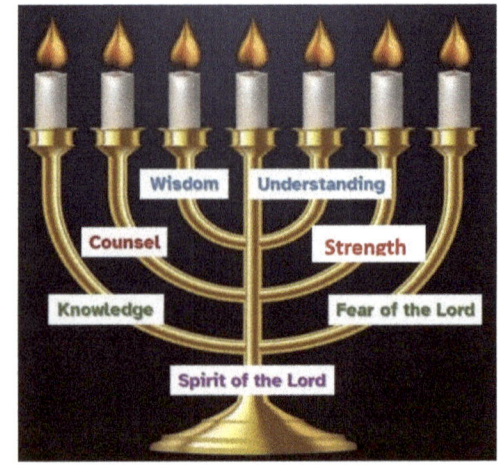

The Menorah provided light for the Holy Place (Jesus Christ is the light of the world). The source of power (oil) for all six lamps was *God*. These 6 gifts supplied the *Spiritual power* and *strength* a person needed to accomplish his or her calling in the Old Testament. These 6 Gifts are briefly defined as follows.

(1) ***Wisdom***   Wisdom is the ability to distinguish right from wrong and to make logical and informed decisions. A wise man will hear and read the Holy Word of God, and increase his/her knowledge of the scriptures.

A man of discernment shall attain unto wise counsel
Proverbs 1:5

(2) ***Understanding***   Understanding is the ability to discern right from wrong

The fear of the LORD is the beginning of wisdom: all who follow after Christ have good understanding   Psalms 111:10

(3) ***Counsel***   Counsel is the ability to receive or give sound advice based upon God's word

A wise man will hear, and will increase learning; and a man of understanding shall attain unto wise counsel   Proverbs 1:5

(4) ***Strength***   Some common synonyms of might are *energy, force, and might*. *Might* implies great or overwhelming power and spiritual strength.

*And he said unto me: My grace is sufficient for thee: for my **strength** is made perfect in weakness*   II Corinthians 12:9

(5) ***Knowledge***   Knowledge is the ability to study and learn; to acquire, retain and master facts and information; and use what is learned to declare that Jesus Christ is Lord and Savior

The heart of the prudent obtains knowledge; and the ear of the wise seeks to hear knowledge   Psalms 18:15

(6) ***Fear of the Lord***   Fear of the Lord is awe, reverence, and respect for God. It acknowledges that everything comes as a gift from God, downplays personal achievement and self-sufficiency, and gladly offers praise, worship, and adoration to God.

If ye will fear the LORD, and serve him, and obey his voice, and not rebel against the commandment of the LORD, then shall both ye and also the King that reigns over you continue following the LORD your God   I Samuel 12:14

The Holy Spirit was part of the eternal Godhead since before the earth was created. The work of the Holy Spirit in the Old Testament can be summarized as follows (Thomas Nelson Bibles).

1 THE SPIRIT PARTICIPATED IN CREATION

The earth was without form, and void; and darkness was on the face of the deep. And the Spirit of God was hovering over the face of the waters. – Genesis 1:2 (NKJV)

2 THE SPIRIT GAVE LIFE TO CREATURES AND THE EARTH

You send forth Your Spirit, they are created; And You renew the face of the earth. – Psalm 104:30 (NKJV)

3 — THE SPIRIT BREATHED LIFE INTO HUMANS

And the LORD God formed man of the dust of the ground, and breathed into his nostrils the breath of life; and man became a living being. – Genesis 2:7 (NKJV)

4 — THE SPIRIT WAS RECOGNIZED BY MEN

And Pharaoh said to his servants, "Can we find such a one as this, a man in whom is the Spirit of God?" – Genesis 41:38 (NKJV)

5 — THE SPIRIT STRIVED WITH SINNERS

And the LORD said, "My Spirit shall not strive with man forever, for he is indeed flesh; yet his days shall be one hundred and twenty years." – Genesis 6:3 (NKJV)

6 — THE SPIRIT GAVE EXTRAORDINARY POWER TO LEADERS

JOSHUA — Numbers 27:18 (NKJV)

OTHNIEL — Judges 3:9-10 (NKJV)

GIDEON — Judges 6:34 (NKJV)

SAMSON — Judges 14:5-6 (NKJV)

SAUL — 1 Samuel 10:9-13 (NKJV)

7. WHEN SAUL DISOBEYED, THE SPIRIT DEPARTED

But the Spirit of the LORD departed from Saul, and a distressing spirit from the LORD troubled him. – 1 Samuel 16:14 (NKJV)

8. THE SPIRIT INSPIRED KING DAVID

The Spirit of the LORD spoke by me, and His word was on my tongue. – 2 Samuel 23:2 (NKJV)

9. THE SPIRIT GUIDED THE PROPHETS

Then the Spirit entered me when He spoke to me, and set me on my feet; and I heard Him who spoke to me. – Ezekiel 2:2 (NKJV)

10. THE SPIRIT INSPIRED HOLINESS

Teach me to do Your will, For You are my God; Your Spirit is good. Lead me in the land of uprightness. – Psalm 143:10 (NKJV)

11. THE SPIRIT ENCOURAGED MORALITY

I will put My Spirit within you and cause you to walk in My statutes, and you will keep My judgments and do them. – Ezekiel 36:27 (NKJV)

12. THE SPIRIT PROPHESIED OF THE MESSIAH

The Spirit of the LORD shall rest upon Him, the Spirit of wisdom and understanding, the Spirit of counsel and might, the Spirit of knowledge and of the fear of the LORD. – Isaiah 11:2 (NKJV)

13. THE SPIRIT IDENTIFIED THE COMING MESSIAH

The Spirit of the Lord GOD is upon Me, Because the LORD has anointed Me to preach good tidings to the poor; He has sent Me to heal the brokenhearted, to proclaim liberty To the captives, And the opening of the prison to those who are bound – Isaiah 61:1 (NKJV)

Chapter 3
The Holy Spirit in the New Testament

In the New Testament, the role of the Holy Spirit is more extensive and personal. Once a person accepts Jesus Christ as their Savior and begins to serve Him in spirit and in truth, that person is *born again*, becomes a new creature in Jesus Christ and is given the Holy Spirit as a guarantee of his /her salvation. We will now describe the uniqueness of the Holy Spirit in the New Testament, and contrast the role of the Holy Spirit under the Old Covenant with the works of the Holy Spirit under the New Covenant.

Each of the gifts of the Holy spirit were available to only a selected few in the *Old Testament*. However, God has empowered each *New Testament* believer to receive one or more gifts which the Holy Spirit will bring to each Born-again Christian.

The role of the Holy Spirit in the New Testament is much more involved in God's eternal plan than it was in the Old Testament. When we speak of the role of the Holy Spirit under the *New Covenant*, we can discern seven general areas in which the Holy Spirit works: (1) *Source* of gifts to carry out the plan of God, (2) *Indwelling* of the Holy Spirit (3) *Filling* of the Holy spirit (4) *Gifts* of the Holy Spirit (5) A *Source of power* for service (6) *Minister* of the *Word of Truth*. (7) *Interpretation and meaning* of the *Word*.

The Holy Spirit embodies the *presence* of God himself who *proceeds* from God the Father.

*Jesus said unto them, If God were your Father, ye would love me: for I **proceed**ed forth and came from God; neither came I of myself, but he sent me*   John 8:42

*But when the **Comforter** is come, whom I will send unto you from the Father, even the **Spirit of Truth**, which **proceedeth** from the Father, he shall testify of me*   John 15:26

The Holy Spirit is a real, spiritual person who indwells and *empowers* God's people in this present age. When Christ was speaking to His disciples on the night before His crucifixion, He explained that He *must go*, but He would always be with them in spirit.

[16] *And I will pray the Father, and he shall give you another Comforter, that he may abide with you forever;*

[17] *Even the Spirit of truth; whom the world cannot receive, because it sees him not, neither knoweth him: but ye know him; for he dwelleth with you, and shall be in you.*

[18] *I will not leave you comfortless: I will come to you*
John 14: 16-18

The Holy Spirit is always referred to as masculine (*He*) in the New Testament. He was called the *paraclete* by John the Apostle. *Paraclete* is a Greek word occurring five times in the Johannine texts of the New Testament. In Christian theology, the word paraclete refers to the Holy Spirit and is translated as *advocate*, *counsellor*, or *helper*.

The Holy Spirit is much more involved in the spiritual life of man in the New Testament than in the Old Testament. We have shown how the *Holy Spirit*……called the *Spirit of God* or just the *Spirit* in the Old Testament …. was given to certain individuals to accomplish the will and eternal plan of God the Father. It is almost certain that the gift of the Holy Spirit was not permanent in the Old Testament, and could be removed by God (Cf…Saul, I Samuel 16:14)). Under the New Covenant, Christ spent 3.5 years teaching, preaching, healing, and announcing that He was the long-awaited Jewish redeemer, who would take away the sins of the world. The completed work of Jesus Christ on the Cross of Calvary was a permanent forgiveness of sins.... past, present and future.

When Jesus Christ died on the Cross, He conquered death, humiliated, and publicly debased Satan, abolished the Law of Moses, and was dead, buried, and resurrected as the Firstfruits of all who would accept Him as the Son of God. He fully accomplished all that He came to do in obedience to God the Father. Salvation was no longer based upon the works of the Law, but would be offered by faith and grace.... first to the Jews at the Feast of Pentecost (Romans 1:16), and then later to the Gentiles (Acts 13:46). The Old Covenant which existed under the Law was finished, the priesthood was finished, and temple worship was finished. The sinful High Priest, who could enter the Holy of Holies in the Temple to plead for the sins of the people only on the Feast of Yom Kippur, was replaced by our perfect and holy Lord and Savior, Jesus Christ. He was the final, sacrificial Lamb of God who shed His precious blood to permanently atone for sin. As our New High Priest, He now sits upon the right-side of God the Father and is our advocate and intercessor (John 14:16, 26; John 15:26; John 16:7).

Through Jesus Christ, we have access to the Father by the *Holy Spirit* (Ephesians 2:18). Death which resulted from any violation of the Old Covenant Law, was replaced by life in our Lord Jesus Christ. The Cross of Calvary *justified* man before God... and eternal life is granted based upon *faith* and grace. How simple and magnificent was God's plan for mankind! However, appropriation of salvation by faith and the Grace of God is not granted automatically. God created each individual to make decisions themselves, and by their own free-will either reject or accept the gift of eternal life by faith. Man is free to follow the sinful ways of the flesh and Satan, or choose holiness and eternal salvation by faith.

Before Christ died, He spent every hour of the day teaching His apostles and His disciples how to spread the gospel. They probably thought that He would establish His eternal kingdom at that time and did not believe that He would be crucified. Knowing that He would not be with them in the flesh, He told them that He would not leave them spiritually, but that He would ask the Father to send them the Holy Spirit.

*... the **Comforter**, which is the Holy Ghost, whom the Father will send in my name, he shall teach you all things, and bring all things to your remembrance, whatsoever I have said unto you*   John 14:26

Jesus Christ was born a Jew, lived as a Jew, and died as a Jew. His ministry of 3.5 years was spoken *only* to Jews (Matthew 10:5, Matthew 15:24). Salvation was offered 1st to the Jews on the Day of Pentecost, and after they rejected Jesus Christ and stoned Stephen, God selected Paul to bring the message of salvation by faith and grace to the Gentiles. Paul revealed this *mystery* in the 13 epistles which he wrote. There is another way to divide the Holy Scriptures which is not widely known among Western Christians.

The entire scope of mankind, from Adam and Eve to the end of the 1000-year Millennial Kingdom, can be divided into 7 separate periods of time called *dispensations*. A dispensation is simply a particular period of time during which God is dealing with mankind in a unique and different manner. Dispensations of recorded time are foreign to almost all Christians, but they are intuitively obvious: The 1st dispensation of time is the *Age of Innocence* which begins with the creation of Adam and Eve and ends when they were expunged from the Garden of Eden. The 7th dispensation of time is the 1000-year *Millennial Kingdom* when Jesus Christ will rule and reign over the Nation of Israel as God had promised to Abraham, Moses, and King David. Even an immature Christian can recognize that these two periods of time are not governed by the same set of rules and regulations (See Phillips, *The Eternal Plan of God*).

The two dispensations of most concern to modern Christians are the (1) *Dispensation of the Law* (The 5th Dispensation) and the (2) *Dispensation of Faith and Grace* (The 6th Dispensation). The Dispensation of the Law was characterized by God, Israel and the 10 Commandments, and The Dispensation of Faith by Jesus Christ, faith, and grace. The Law was good and it was holy… it was established by God to bring salvation and eternal life to His chosen people the Jews: However, the law was flawed in that no one could ever live under the Law in a sinful body inherited from Adam's seed. The flesh was weak and could never fulfill the law. Hence, the Law both defined sin and brought death. The law could not save anyone, so God had to do something. Throughout the Old Testament, the prophets all prophesied that one day a *Messiah* would arise… sent by God… who would redeem them from sin. John the Baptist was a man who prepared the way for that Messiah who would be called *Jesus the Christ* (Matthew 1:21). He would come to take away the sins of the world; past, present, and future). John baptized Jews into *repentance* to prepare them for the physical appearance of their long-awaited Messiah. In the Fall of 26 AD John was baptizing in the River Jordan when he looked up and announced:

*Behold the **Lamb of God**, which taketh away the sin of the world*
John 1:29

Jesus Christ had arrived to bring forgiveness of sin and redemption to God's beloved people… Israel. John's baptism was by water and it was a baptism to *repentance*.

Repent *ye: for the kingdom of heaven is at hand*   Matthew 3:10

He prepared Israel for the arrival of Jesus Christ, and His message of reconciliation. Jesus Christ taught, healed, and declared Himself to be the Son of God by miracles, healing, control over the very forces of nature, and by resurrection from the grave. Jesus Christ was *born* sinless under the Law. He was the Son of God, and only He could *live* a sinless life under the Law. In the Spring of 30 AD on the Jewish Feast of Passover, Christ was crucified as the perfect, sinless Lamb of God. As a result of His sinless sacrifice and suffering, He shed His precious blood and paid the price for our sins. Sinful man could stand before God fully justified. Salvation and eternal life were no longer denied by sin in sinful man. The work of the Cross was to forgive all sins and not save sinful man. Salvation is now granted to sinful man not by the works of the Law, but by *faith*… Faith that Jesus Christ was the Son of God. As the Son of Man, He came to earth clothed in a perishable human body. He was crucified, dead and buried; and He arose from the grave after 3 days and 3 nights. He presented Himself to God as the perfect, sacrificial Lamb of God. He now sits on the right-hand-side of God the Father, constantly making intercession for all who would believe. God accepted all this, and appropriates salvation and eternal life by His unending, and boundless grace. HALLALEUA and PRAISE GOD Forever.

It is important to once again recognize that Jesus Christ was born a Jew…lived His entire life as a Jew… and died as a Jew. His entire earthly ministry was to the Jews. In fact, He specifically commanded His disciples to not speak to the Gentiles.

*These twelve Jesus sent forth, and commanded them, saying: Go not into the way of the **Gentile**s, and into any city of the Samaritans enter ye not* Matthew 10:5

The Holy Bible as we know it today is divided into an *Old Testament* and a *New Testament*. The dividing line between the Old and New Testaments was when Christ began His earthly ministry and was baptized by John at the River Jordan. The Gospel accounts of Matthew, Mark, Luke, and John are written records of the 3.5-year ministry of Christ. This ministry was *only* to the Jews and not to the Gentiles. This ministry was to fulfil all Old Testament prophecy that a man (Jesus Christ) who would be sent from God would someday arise to redeem the sins of Israel. However, the Gospel accounts of Matthew, Mark, Luke, and John should be the last 4 books of the Old Testament, and the Book of Acts is a transition between the Old Covenant and the New Covenant.

Authors note: The Authorized King James version of the Holy Bible contains 66 books. The Roman Catholic Bible contains 73 books; the additional seven books are called the Apocrypha and are considered canonical by the Catholic Church, but not by other Christians.

The New Covenant was a *Mystery* which was not known until Saul of Tarsus (Paul) was chosen to bring salvation to Jews and Gentiles alike. The correct organization of the 66 Books in the King James Bible should be as shown in the following graphic.

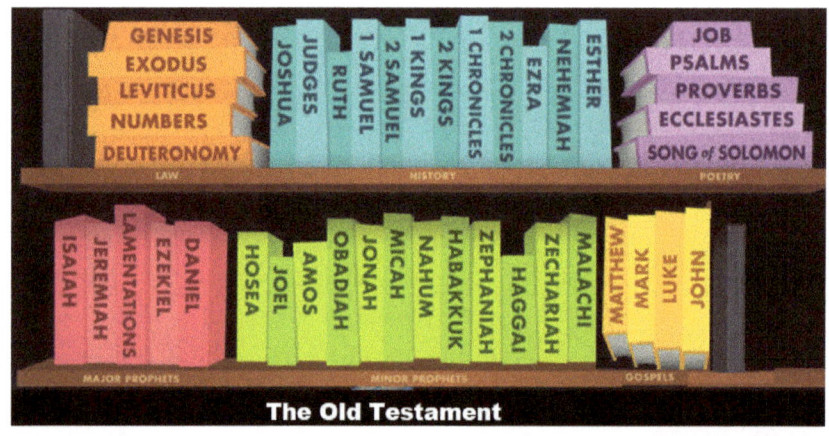

Once this is understood, the things which took place 50 days after the Crucifixion of Christ on the Day of Pentecost… and crucial role of how the Holy Spirit operates in the New Covenant now fall into place.

The Day of Pentecost

When John baptized Christ (with water) he boldly declared to all:

[30] *This is he of whom I said, After me cometh a man which is preferred before me: for he was before me.*
[31] *And I knew him not: but that he should be made manifest to Israel, therefore am I come baptizing with water.*
[32] *And John bare record, saying, I saw the Spirit descending from heaven like a dove, and it abode upon him.*
[33] *And I knew him not: but he that sent me to baptize with water, the same said unto me,* **Upon whom thou shalt see the Spirit descending, and remaining on him, the same is he which baptizes with the Holy Ghost.** John 1: 30-33

I indeed baptize you with water unto repentance: but he that cometh after me is mightier than I, whose shoes I am not worthy to bear: **he shall baptize you with the Holy Ghost, and with fire**
Matthew 3:11

Both John and Matthew are two witnesses to the prophecy that *Jesus Christ will baptize you with the Holy Ghost.* Who is **you** in Matthew 3:11? Those whom Christ will be baptized with the **Holy Ghost** are not Gentiles, but **Jews**. Matthew wrote that Christ would not baptize the Jews with water, but with the Holy Ghost (*Holy Spirit*) and with *fire*. John and Matthew were not speaking to us today and is not directing truth to the Gentiles or the church (body of Christ) today, but to the Jews the church (current Christians) was still a Mystery which had not yet been revealed by Paul…. It was totally unknown. So: *When did these prophecies come to pass?*

Consider what happened in John 20: 1-31. Jesus had risen from the dead, presented Himself to the Father as the final and perfect sacrifice as the Lamb of God, and was now ready to return and speak to His apostles and disciples: Charging them with spreading the Gospel message throughout the known world. As they (apostles and disciples) were gathered and hiding for *fear of the Jews* (John 20: 19,24), Jesus suddenly appeared and saluted them with *peace be unto you.*

And when he had said this, he breathed on them, and saith unto them, Receive ye the Holy Ghost John 20:22

Jesus had previously told His apostles to meet Him in Jerusalem 50 days after He had risen from the grave. It was then that that the promise of the Holy Spirit would take place to fulfill the prophetic words of the Jewish Prophet, Joel.

[16] But this is that which was spoken by the prophet Joel;
[17] And it shall come to pass in the last days, saith God, I will pour out of my Spirit upon all flesh Acts 2:17

There is an apparent conflict between John 20:22 and Acts 2:17. In the event documented in John 20:22, Jesus does not give them the full gift of the Holy Spirit - which they will receive at Pentecost... but only that which they will require for the purpose of remitting the sins of others (John 20:23).

Until the day in which he was taken up, after that he through the Holy Ghost, He had given commandments unto the apostles whom he had chosen Acts 1:2

Jesus Christ commissioned His disciples to go forth in John 20:22 led by the Holy Spirit which was in Him (Matthew 3:16). This was only a *partial infilling* of the Holy Spirit. On the day of Pentecost (remember that a Jewish day starts at 6:00 PM), there were 120 apostles and disciples gathered. Christ had told His apostles to meet Him in Jerusalem… BE THERE.

[46] *And said unto them, Thus it is written, and thus it behooved Christ to suffer, and to rise from the dead the third day:*
[47] *And that repentance and remission of sins should be preached in his name among all nations, beginning at Jerusalem.*
[48] *And ye are witnesses of these things.*
[49] *And, behold, I send the promise of my Father upon you: but tarry ye in the city of Jerusalem, until ye be endued with power from on high*
Luke 24: 46-49

[1] *And when the day of Pentecost was fully come, they were all with one accord in one place.*
[2] *And suddenly there came a sound from heaven as of a rushing mighty wind, and it* **filled all the house** *where they were sitting.*
[3] *And there appeared unto them cloven tongues like as of fire, and it sat upon each of them*   Acts 2: 1-3

This outpouring of the Holy Spirit in Acts 2: 1-3 appears to confirm that 120 Jews received the Holy Spirit on the evening before the Feast of Pentecost (Jewish days begin at 6:00 PM). Luke goes on to say that news of this event quickly spread to other Jews in Jerusalem who were there to attend the Feast.

[5] *And there were dwelling at Jerusalem Jews, devout men, out of every nation under heaven.*
[6] *Now when this was noised abroad, the multitude came together, and were confounded, because that every man heard them speak in his own language.*
[7] *And they were all amazed and marveled, saying one to another, Behold, are not all these which speak Galileans?*

[8] *And how hear we **every man in our own tongue, wherein we were born?*** Acts 2: 5-8

Peter arose and preached to those who had gathered there that this was prophesied long ago by the prophet Joel (Acts 2:14-21).

[38] *Then Peter said unto them, Repent, and be baptized every one of you in the name of Jesus Christ for the remission of sins, and ye shall receive the gift of the Holy Ghost.*

[39] *For the promise is unto you, and to your children, and to all that are afar off, even as many as the Lord our God shall call.*

[40] *And with many other words did he testify and exhort, saying, Save yourselves from this untoward generation.*

[41] *Then they that gladly received his word were baptized: and **the same day there were added unto them about three thousand souls*** Acts 2: 38-41

The total of 3000 souls were saved, in addition to the 120 that previously received the Holy Spirit (Acts 1:15). It is interesting that the first group of 120 to receive the Holy Spirit after the death of Christ was symbolic of the 120 priests who were with Solomon when he brought the Ark of the Covenant to Jerusalem. The Ark of the Covenant in the Old Covenant symbolized God's Presence *among men* (2 Chron 5:12). The Holy Spirit was the fulfillment of this type. The Holy Spirit is God dwelling *in men* under the New Covenant. The 3000 Jews who received the Holy Spirit on the Day of Pentecost also were also an antitype of a type. When Moses descended from Mt Sinai with the Law that God had written, it angered so much that He killed 3000 Israelites who had made a Golden Calf. Here again we see a hidden message in scripture. The *Law* and the *Old Covenant* brought *death*, but *faith* and a *New Covenant* brought *life*.

Note that the Feast of Pentecost **was not** the birthday of the *Church* as many claim. The events which took place on the Day of Pentecost were to fulfill the words of the prophet Joel, and did not involve any Gentiles. The risen Jesus Christ caused the Holy Spirit to fall with tongues of fire upon 3000 Jews who were gathered there. After Paul revealed the Mystery of the New Covenant, the Holy Spirit fell upon *all* Born-again believers. The *church* is a poor descriptor in modern times… it should be recognized as a *building*. All true believers who we call Christians who gather in a building are the *ecclesia* or the *body of Christ.* Note that the New Covenant body of believers had not yet been revealed by Paul. The body of true believers which would consist of *both* Jews and Gentiles was still a *mystery*. Forgiveness of sins by the accomplished work of Jesus Christ that freed the Jews from the Curse of the Law meant that all Jews (past and present) cold receive eternal life by the Faith of Abraham. All Old Covenant Jews were saved in the same way that all Jews and Gentiles are saved under the New Covenant…. By *faith*.

The Holy Spirit and Salvation
Most Christians fail to understand the critical role that the Holy Spirit plays in New Covenant Salvation. Under the Old Covenant, salvation was based upon obeying the Law which God had given to Moses and Israel at Mt. Sinai.

And it shall come to pass, if thou shalt hearken diligently unto the voice of the LORD thy God, to observe and to do all his commandments which I command thee this day, that the LORD thy God will set thee on high above all nations of the earth   Deuteronomy 28:1

Obey every part of the Law and live; trespass against only one commandment in the law and die (Deuteronomy 4).

For as many as have sinned without law shall also perish without law: and as many as have sinned in the law shall be judged by the law
    Romans 2:12

*Therefore, by the deeds of the **law** there shall no flesh be justified in his sight: for by the **law** is the knowledge of sin*   Romans 3:20

For whosoever shall keep the whole law, and yet offend in one point, he is guilty of all.   James 2:10

[10] For as many as are of the works of the law are under the curse: for it is written, Cursed is every one that continues not in all things which are written in the book of the law to do them.
[11] But that no man is justified by the law in the sight of God, it is evident: The just shall live by faith   Galatians 10:11

The Holy Spirit is not just a power gift which is given to Christians today (Acts 1:8), but the Holy Spirit is necessary to obtain eternal life in Christ Jesus. This is a concept that is seldom taught in the pulpit or expounded upon in studies of the Holy Spirit.

*[5] Jesus answered, Verily, verily, I say unto thee: Except a man be born of water and of the **Spirit**, he cannot enter into the kingdom of God.* John 3: 5

Paul was a 2nd witness to the words written by John.

*But ye are not in the flesh, but in the **Spirit**, if so be that the **Spirit** of God dwell in you. Now if any man has not the **Spirit** of Christ, **he is none of his***   Romans 8:9

The Holy Spirit (Spirit of God) was desired in the Old Testament, but was only given to certain individuals by God Himself. When Paul announced the mystery of the New Covenant, he made it clear that the Holy Spirit would come upon each true believer when that person chooses to live a new life in Christ. Upon deciding to die to the world, live in Jesus Christ, and obey His commands… the Holy Spirit immediately begins to dwell in that person. This transformation into a new creature in Christ is called being *Born-again*.

In John 3:1 a leader of the Jews called Nicodemus came to Jesus by night. He perceived that Jesus was a man sent by God, and he wanted to know how he could obtain eternal life.

[3] *Jesus answered and said unto him, Verily, verily, I say unto thee:* **Except a man be born again, he cannot see the kingdom of God**.

Nicodemus was obviously confused, and he asked: *Can a man be born of his mother again?*

[4] *Nicodemus saith unto him: How can a man be born when he is old? can he enter the second time into his mother's womb, and be born?*

Jesus immediately responded that any man who seeks salvation and eternal life must be first born by a woman (water), and then be born again spiritually (Spirit birth).

[5] *Jesus answered, Verily, verily, I say unto thee, except a man be born of water and of the Spirit, he cannot enter into the kingdom of God.*
[6] *That which is born of the flesh is flesh; and that which is born of the Spirit is spirit*   John 3: 5-6

Paul later explained exactly what Christ had told Nicodemus. Water is a necessary part natural birth that all humans experience. The spirit birth Is defined as that work whereby the Holy Spirit places the believer into union with Christ, and into union with other believers in the body of Christ, at the moment of being Born-Again.

For John truly baptized with water; but ye shall be baptized with the Holy Ghost not many days hence: For John baptized with water, but in a few days you will be baptized with the Holy Spirit   Acts 1:5

This promise was first fulfilled on the Day of Pentecost (Acts 2:1–4), and for the first time, Jews were permanently indwelt by the Holy Spirit. Christ then told Nicodemus:

Marvel not that I said unto thee, Ye must be born again   John 3:7

There is no ambiguity or room for misunderstanding the words of Christ: *YOU MUST BE BORN AGAIN*. Please notice once again that Jesus was a Jew who was speaking to another Jew. Note what John said after He baptized Jesus into His 3.5-year ministry.

*And I knew him not: but he that sent me to baptize with water, the same said unto me: Upon whom thou shalt see the Spirit descending, and remaining on him, **the same is he which baptizes with the Holy Ghost*** John 1:33

Matthew later added the following in a parallel record.

*I indeed baptize you with water unto repentance: but he that cometh after me is mightier than I, whose shoes I am not worthy to bear: **He** shall baptize you with the Holy Ghost, and with fire*   Matthew 3:11

The apostle Paul clearly taught that we receive the Holy Spirit the moment we receive Jesus Christ as our Savior.

*For **we were all baptized by one Spirit** into one body—whether Jews or Greeks, slave or free—and we were all given the one Spirit to drink* I Corinthians 12:13

This one spirit is the Holy Spirit, who is also our *guarantee* of salvation. He is also our *deposit* which seals our promised inheritance.

*Having believed, you were marked in him with a seal, the promised Holy Spirit, who is a **deposit** guaranteeing our inheritance until the redemption of those who are God's possession—to the praise of his glory* Ephesians 1:13-14

There is an apparent contradiction in what Matthew wrote in Matthew 3:11 and what Paul wrote in I Corinthians 12:13 concerning *spiritual baptism*. Matthew said **Jesus Christ** would baptize *with fire and the Holy Ghost* (Matthew 3:11). This was clearly fulfilled on the Day of Pentecost 50 days after His resurrection. Paul later wrote that the **Holy Ghost** would baptize all born-again believers into Christ (I Corinthians 12:13). Careful exegesis of the Holy Scriptures reveal that there is no contradiction. Jesus fulfilled the prophecy of John the Baptist, which was spoken to Jews at the River Jordan. *Pentecost* was a Jewish Feast ordained by God to the Jews. The Jews are God's chosen people, and salvation by faith and grace was 1st offered to the Jews on the Feast of Pentecost in Jerusalem (Romans 1:16). The resurrected Christ baptized 3000 Jews on the Feast of Pentecost *with* the Holy Spirit (Acts 2:41). Paul later revealed the *mystery* of the *New Covenant*, which offered salvation to Jews and Gentiles alike…. All who would believe upon the Christ and be Born-again. Once either a Jew or Gentile accepts Jesus Christ as their Lord and Savior, a series of remarkable spiritual transformations take place. When born-again that person: (1) Receives the Holy Spirit (2) dies to the world (3) lives in Jesus Christ and (4) Becomes a new creature in Jesus Christ. Paul describes this new creature as a Born-again believer who has *put on* Jesus Christ.

*For as many of you as have been baptized into Christ have **put on Christ***   Galatians 3:27

His /her natural birth into the Old Adam becomes a spiritual birth into the New Adam…. Jesus Christ. A person is baptized into the body of Jesus Christ (spiritually) by the Holy Spirit. This is clearly not the same as Jesus Christ baptizing new Jewish believers with the Holy Spirit at Pentecost. Pentecost was the fulfillment of all Old Testament prophecy concerning redemption and salvation by faith for all Old Jewish believers who were at the Feast of Pentecost. At the Feast of Pentecost, the resurrected Jesus Christ baptized 3000 Jews with the Holy Spirit. Under the New Covenant, at the moment that any Christian is Born-again, that person receives the Holy Spirit and becomes a member of the body of Christ. This spiritual baptism is not *by Christ*, but is *into Christ* by the Holy Spirit. Paul explained this in his letters to the church members at Corinth.

[12] For as the body is one, and hath many members, and all the members of that one body, being many, are one body: so also, is Christ.
*[13] For **by one Spirit are we all baptized into one body**, whether we be Jews or Gentiles, whether we be bond or free; and have been all made to drink into one spirit*   I Corinthians 12: 12-13

[17] Therefore if any man be in Christ, he is a new creature: old things are passed away; behold, all things are become new.
[18] And all things are of God, who hath reconciled us to himself by Jesus Christ, and hath given to us the ministry of reconciliation;
[19] To wit, that God was in Christ, reconciling the world unto himself, not imputing their trespasses unto them; and hath committed unto us the word of reconciliation.
[20] Now then we are ambassadors for Christ, as though God did beseech you by us: we pray you in Christ's stead, be ye reconciled to God.
[21] For he hath made him to be sin for us, who knew no sin; that we might be made the righteousness of God in him   II Corinthians 5: 17-21

Becoming the *new creature* begins at the moment of being Born-again, when we accept Christ's gift of salvation and are *justified* (I Corinthians 6:11; Ephesians 2:13). Before Christ finished His work on the Cross of Calvary, we were *dead* because of our sins and because of our sinful nature under the Law. After Jesus Christ was raised from the dead, ascended to heaven, and asked the Father to send the Holy Spirit to all Born-again believers… we are made *alive* in Jesus Christ by faith.

And you, being dead in your sins and the uncircumcision of your flesh, hath he quickened together with him, having forgiven you all trespasses Colossians 2:13

Our *old man*… our unregenerated, sinful selves… is crucified, dead, and buried with Christ when we accept Him as our Lord and Savior. We become a *new man* raised to new life in Christ (I Corinthians 6:11; Romans 6: 4–6; Galatians 2:20). From then on, the process of *sanctification* continues for the rest of our life.

The Holy Spirit begins to renew our minds, thoughts, and attitudes; changing us and shaping us to be more like Jesus Christ (Romans 12:2; Ephesians 4:23; II Corinthians 3:18). As we spend time in prayer, grow in the grace, acquire knowledge of Him, and study His Word: We become: *in every way more and more like Christ, who is the head of his body, the church* (John 17:17, Ephesians 5: 25–26, II Timothy 3:16).

The Holy Spirit (Holy Ghost) is much more active in every true believer under the New Covenant than it was under the Old Covenant. Christ told his disciples that He must go but that He would not leave them comfortless (spiritually). He promised that the Spirit of Truth (the Holy Spirit) would be with them *forever*.

[16] *And I will pray the Father, and he shall give you another* **Comforter** (Paraclete), *that he may abide with you* ***forever***;
[17] *Even the Spirit of truth; whom the world cannot receive, because it sees him not, neither knoweth him: but ye know him; for he dwelleth with you, and shall be in you.*
[18] ***I will not leave you comfortless****: I will come to you*
John 14: 16-18

The Holy Spirit assumes multiple roles of great importance once He is sent to reside in every Born-again believer. The following is a partial list of the roles that the Holy Spirit assumes in a Born-Again Christian.

- He leads and directs workers in their ministry (Acts 8:29; 10:19-20; 16:6-7; 1 Corinthians 2:13),
- He speaks through prophets (Acts 1:16; 1 Peter 1:11-12; 2 Peter 1:21),
- He corrects (John 16:8),
- He comforts (Acts 9:31),
- He helps heal our infirmities (Romans 8:26),
- He teaches us all things (John 14:26; 1 Corinthians 12:3),
- He guides us in our spiritual journey through life (John 16:13),
- He sanctifies us as we mature and grow spiritually (Romans 15:16; 1 Corinthians 6:11),
- He testifies of Christ (John 15:26), and glorifies Christ (John 16:14),
- He empowers all Born-again believers to carry out the work which has been assigned to us (Romans 15:13),
- He reveals the wisdom and knowledge of God (Romans 11: 33-34, I Corinthians 2: 1-11),
- He distributes Gifts of the Holy Spirit to Born-again believers (I Corinthians 12:11),
- He dwells within the ecclesia (John 14:17),
- He can be grieved (Ephesians 4:30),
- He can be resisted (Acts 7:51)
- He can be tempted by Satan and unbelievers (Acts 5:9).

The Gift *of the Holy Spirit*

A Born-Again Christian is expected to live within and for Christ as members of His body here on earth. The Holy Spirit brings gifts to all who have been regenerated and become a new creature in Christ. These gifts sustain, support, and lead all Born-again Christians to boldly preach the gospel message and complete the work pre-ordained for them.

The New Testament has much to say about the role of the Holy Spirit in a true believer's life. Any Christian will recognize the rightful place of the Holy Spirit as a member of the eternal triad of God the Father, Jesus Christ the Son, and the Holy Spirit. We will characterize and explain the Holy Spirit within every New Covenant believer under 3 broad categories: (1) The *Presence* of the Holy Spirit in every believer (2) The *Purpose* of the Holy Spirit in every born-again Christian and (3) The *Power* of the Holy Spirit.

Presence of the Holy Spirit

When Christ spoke to His apostles just before He was arrested and crucified, He told them the following:

[7] *Nevertheless I tell you the truth; It is expedient for you that I go away: for if I go not away, the Comforter will not come unto you; but if I depart, I will send him unto you.*

[8] *And when he is come, he will reprove the world of sin, and of righteousness, and of judgment:*

[9] *Of sin, because they believe not on me;*

[10] *Of righteousness, because I go to my Father, and ye see me no more;*

[11] *Of judgment, because the prince of this world is judged.*

[12] *I have yet many things to say unto you, but ye cannot bear them now.*

[13] *Howbeit when he, the Spirit of truth, is come, he will guide you into all truth: for he shall not speak of himself; but whatsoever he shall hear, that shall he speak: and he will shew you things to come.*

[14] *He shall glorify me: for he shall receive of mine, and shall shew it unto you*   John 16: 7-14

Jesus Christ promised His disciples that He would not leave them helpless, but that after He is gone, He would send them the great *comforter*, which is another term for the *Holy Spirit*. This first happened to Jewish born-again believers on the *Day of Pentecost*, when the Holy Spirit fell upon each apostle, and 3000 other Jews who had gathered in Jerusalem. After salvation was offered first to the Jews, Jesus turned to the Gentiles and anointed Paul to reveal the *mystery* of the New Covenant. The Holy Spirit is *omnipresent*. King David acknowledged this when he asked:

[7] *Whither shall I go from thy spirit? or whither shall I flee from thy presence?*
[8] *If I ascend up into heaven, thou art there: if I make my bed in hell, behold, thou art there.*
[9] *If I take the wings of the morning, and dwell in the uttermost parts of the sea*
[10] *Even there shall thy hand lead me, and thy right hand shall hold me*
Psalms 139: 7-9

This is possible because, unlike humans, the Holy Spirit is not flesh and blood but a *Spirit*. The Holy Spirit conceived Jesus Christ. We rarely consider the profound implications of Matthew 1:

[18] *Now the birth of Jesus Christ was on this wise: When as his mother Mary was espoused to Joseph, before they came together, she was found with child of the Holy Ghost.*
[19] *Then Joseph her husband, being a just man, and not willing to make her a public example, was minded to put her away privily.*
[20] *But while he thought on these things, behold, the angel of the Lord appeared unto him in a dream, saying, Joseph, thou son of David, fear not to take unto thee Mary thy wife: for that which is conceived in her is of the Holy Ghost.*   Matthew 1: 18-20

It was part of God's eternal plan to send Jesus Christ to earth to redeem sinful man, and to initiate the New Covenant by which both Jews and

Gentiles are saved by faith and grace. This could never have happened without the role of the Holy Spirit in the birth of mother Mary. Jesus would have been born with the curse of Adam if born through normal intercourse like every other man or woman, Jesus, would have been cursed by the original sin of Adam. By being conceived through a supernatural process, Jesus Christ was born sinless and lived a sinless life under the Law. He was the only person born of woman who could redeem the entire world from all sins. He was the perfect Lamb of God who was accepted as the last and complete sacrifice for sin.

The Holy spirit helps us *understand* all things; He *guides us* when we need discernment and wisdom; He *leads us* when we need to discern right from wrong, and He *convicts* us when we need to reject sinful acts. The Holy Spirit *reveals* to us God's truth, and God's truth *renews our conscience.*

He will give you another Helper, that He may be with you forever
John 14:16

[10] *But God hath revealed them unto us by his Spirit: for the Spirit searches all things, yea, the deep things of God.*
[11] *For what man knoweth the things of a man, save the spirit of man which is in him? even so the things of God knoweth no man, but the Spirit of God.*
[12] *Now we have received, not the spirit of the world, but the spirit which is of God; that we might know the things that are freely given to us of God.*
[13] *Which things also we speak, not in the words which man's wisdom teaches, but which the Holy Ghost teaches; comparing spiritual things with spiritual*   I Corinthians 2: 10-13

The *Purpose* of the Holy Spirit

As a part of the New Covenant, the Holy Spirit is promised to everyone who becomes a Born-again Christian. There are several specific *Mental* and *Spiritual* transformations which take place when anyone decides to give their life to Jesus Christ.

- The word is *received*
- The word is *believed*
- The person surrenders their life to Jesus Christ and is *born again.*
- The Holy Spirit is sent to *dwell* in every new Born-again Christian

The Phrase *Born-again* is first used by Christ in John 3:3. A ruler of the Jews called Nicodemus had evidently heard the gospel message, and he wanted to believe. He came to Jesus by night and spoke:
Rabbi, we know that thou art a teacher come from God: for no man can do these miracles that thou doest, except God be with him
John 3:2

Jesus Christ, knowing the true thoughts and heart of all men, perceived that the man wanted to accept Him as the Son of God and his redeemer He responded:

Verily, verily, I say unto thee: **Except a man be born again**, *he cannot see the Kingdom of God*   John 3:3

This must have startled and confused Nicodemus because he then asked:

How can a man be born when he is old? can he enter the second time into his mother's womb, and be born?   John 3:4

Jesus then told Nicodemus:
[6] *That which is born of the flesh is flesh; and that which is born of the Spirit is Spirit.*
[7] *Marvel not that I said unto thee,* **Ye must be born again**.
[8] *The wind blows where it will, and you hear the sound, but cannot tell whence it cometh, and whither it goeth: so is every one that is born of the Spirit.*
[9] *Nicodemus answered and said unto him, How can these things be?*
[10] *Jesus answered and said unto him, Art thou a master of Israel, and knowest not these things?*   John 3: 8-10

Jesus rebuked Nicodemus and told him: *You are a ruler of the Jews and do not know these things?* Nicodemus had previously asked; *How can these things be?* Jesus had already revealed the truth of how He responded to Nicodemus.

[12] *But as many as received him, to them he gave power to become the sons of God, even to them that believe on his name*:
[13] *Which were born, not of blood, nor of the will of the flesh, nor of the will of man, but of God.*   John 3: 12-13

The phrase *Born-again* means to be reborn *Spiritually*. Nicodemus needed a change in his heart…... a Spiritual transformation. He needed to experience birth into a new creature who would be conformed to the image and will of Jesus Christ, not his own. Being Born-again is an act of God, and eternal life is promised to the person who believes (I Corinthians 5:17; Titus 3:5; I Peter 1:3; I John 2:29; 3:9; 4:7; 5:1-4, 18). John 1: 12,13). Being born again also involves becoming a Son of God by trusting in the name of Jesus Christ. *How does this transformation take place?* The gifts of the Holy Spirit are to edify and nurture the Body of Christ, to build up the *ecclesia*, and to teach salvation to both immature believers and unbelievers. Christ taught that this was a holy calling for all who seek to win souls to Jesus Christ until *all* reach unity in the faith and become mature, attaining to a complete measure of the fullness of Christ (Ephesians 4: 12–13). This will not be achieved until Christ Returns a 2nd time and the Age of Faith and Grace ends.

For now we see through a glass, darkly; but then face to face: now I know in part; but then shall I know even as also I am known
I Corinthians 13:12

Each person upon accepting Jesus Christ as redeemer, savior and Son of God is Born-again and receives the Holy Spirit as a *seal of salvation* (Ephesians 1:12–14). The Spirit then begins to reside in each true believer and grants certain gifts from God to do the work of Jesus Christ (I Corinthians 12: 4–6).

Spiritual gifts should *never* be used to draw attention to oneself or put on a personal display. This was part of the problem in the church in Corinth. Some of the new Christians in the Church at Corinth had used their new spiritual freedom to hold themselves up as *special* and *chosen*. They mistreated *baby and immature Christians* within that same community. Divisions erupted among believers, and sin began to infiltrate what was once a Holy and dedicated community. *All things are lawful*, some of the members maintained, claiming that they had carte blanche to behave as they wished. Members there were doing as they pleased, abusing the forgiveness of sins which Christ had accomplished on the Cross of Calvary. Paul had already warned them of such behavior, but they had ignored his warning.

[1] *What shall we say then? Shall we continue in sin, that grace may abound?*
[2] *God forbid. How shall we, that are dead to sin, live any longer therein?*
[15] *What then? shall we sin, because we are not under the law, but under grace? God forbid*   Romans 6: 1-2, 15

These Christians in Corinth were exercising their spiritual gifts to edify themselves without regard to what anyone else was doing (I Corinthians 14:4), and their methods resulted in chaos in the church service (I Corinthians 14:23, 27–28). They needed to be reminded that the greatest gift of all is *love* (I Corinthians 13:13) and that no gift should be used unless it edifies both believers and unbelievers. Without love, none of the gifts are profitable at all (I Corinthians 13:1–3). All gifts are given by God through the Holy Spirit (Romans 12:6; I Corinthians 12:4; Hebrews 2:4). Different people are given different gifts. Not everyone receives exactly the same gift (I Corinthians 12:4), and it is rare that anyone possesses all the gifts. Those gifted with various spiritual gifts are meant to work together as the parts of a body work together (I Corinthians 12:12–27). The gifts that the Holy Spirit imparts to a born-again believer divinely dispersed for the good of the body of Christ exactly when that particular gift is activated (I Corinthians 12:27). We should always exercise and develop the special gifts that God has given us.

[38] *For I am persuaded, that neither death, nor life, nor angels, nor principalities, nor powers, nor things present, nor things to come,* [39] *Nor height, nor depth, nor any other creature, shall be able to separate us from the love of God, which is in Christ Jesus our Lord* Romans 8: 38-39

Power *of* the Holy Spirit
The average Christian does not fully understand or recognize the *power* which is given to each individual by the Holy Spirit. *Every Christian* is given the gift of the Holy Spirit when they accept Him as their Lord and Savior and is Born-again. The Holy Spirit baptizes each born-again Christian into the body of Jesus Christ, and then bestows upon that individual gifts from on high by which every Christian can function in a world of sin and unrighteousness. This is the victory that we have in Jesus Christ.

Jesus promised the Holy Spirit as a permanent guide, teacher, seal of salvation, and comforter for believers (John 14:16-18). He also promised that the Holy Spirit's *power* would help His followers to spread the message of the gospel around the world: *But you will receive power when the Holy Spirit comes on you; and you will be my witnesses in Jerusalem, and in all Judea and Samaria, and to the ends of the earth* (Acts 1:8). The salvation of souls is a supernatural work only made possible by the Holy Spirit's power at work in the world.

For our gospel came not unto you in word only, but also in power, and in the Holy Ghost, and in much assurance; as ye know what manner of men we were among you for your sake   I Thessalonians 1:5

The power of the Holy Spirit is literally authority granted from God, which is infinite, unlimited, and eternal. In this way, the power of the Holy Spirit is different from any other kind of power. Since God alone is omnipotent, the power which is given to each individual through the Holy Spirit is limited to the calling and execution of corresponding gifts. The Apostle Paul gave all the credit and glory to the presence and intervention of the Holy Spirit, whose power enabled his message to pierce the hearts of sinful men and bring them to salvation. He knew it was not his apologetics, hermeneutics, or persuasive ability that brought people to Christ but the power of the Holy Spirit.

[4] And my speech and my preaching was not with enticing words of man's wisdom, but in demonstration of the Spirit and of power:
[5] That your faith should not stand in the wisdom of men, but in the power of God.   I Corinthians 2: 4-5

Baptism *by* the Holy Spirit

The Agent by which a person is Born-again is by the *Holy Spirit*. Once a person believes and accepts Jesus Christ as their Lord and Savior, they immediately receive the gift of the Holy Spirit from God the Father at the request of Jesus Christ. It is by and through the Holy Spirit that a person is *baptized into the body of Christ*. Paul explained this when he revealed the *mystery* of the New Covenant.

*For **by one Spirit are we all baptized into one body**, whether we be Jews or Gentiles, whether we be bond or free; and have been all made to drink into one Spirit*   I Corinthians 12:13

The *Holy Spirit* is the Spiritual vehicle by which every true Christian is baptized into the Body of Christ, He also It is not unusual for new Christians to identify water with this baptism. Baptism by water is not always implied whenever the word *baptism* is encountered in the Holy Scriptures. The baptism into Christ by the Holy Spirit is not physical but *spiritual*. The Holy Spirit is the agent or vehicle through which a new believer is baptized into Jesus Christ. This is what John the Baptist spoke of when He baptized Christ with water in the River Jordan.

And I knew him not: but he that sent me to baptize with water, the same said unto me: Upon whom thou shalt see the Spirit descending, and remaining on him, the same is he which baptizes with the Holy Ghost
John 1:33

This is not the cleansing baptism of the Old Covenant or John's baptism of repentance, but a new supernatural, spiritual birth. Part of that spiritual transformation is to receive forgiveness of all sin and become a New Adam…. The Old Adam has passed away. That is why Paul said:

Therefore, if any man be in Christ, he is a new creature: old things are passed away; behold, all things are become new.
II Corinthians 5:17

[22] *For as in Adam all die, even so in Christ shall all be made alive.*
[45] *And so it is written: The first man Adam was made a living soul; the last Adam was made a quickening spirit*
I Corinthians 15: 22, 45
For as many of you as have been baptized into Christ have put on Christ
Galatians 3:27

Baptism by the Holy Spirit can also be defined as that work whereby at the moment of salvation the Spirit of God places the believer into union with Christ, and into a common Spiritual body with other believers. There is confusion among Christians as to the difference between a person being baptized *into* Christ by the Holy Spirit and the action of being baptized *with the* Holy Spirit to carry out the work of the ministry of Jesus Christ.

Baptism *of* the Holy Spirit
The baptism *of the Holy Spirit* was predicted by John the Baptist (Mark 1:8) and by Jesus before He ascended to heaven (Acts 1:5).

For John baptized with water, but in a few days, you will be baptized with the Holy Spirit   Acts 1:5

We should then exercise our Spiritual gifts to keep the body of Christ functioning properly.   https://www.gotquestions.org/

The following comments were extracted in large part from Bill Brinkworth https://www.devotionsfromthebible.com/exodus/i-cant-but-he-can/ ,who eloquently states what a Born-again believer can do.

> God does not ask anyone to do anything that they cannot do. If God enters a person's heart to do something, it can be done! Maybe not on their own; maybe not without God's help; but if God calls a person to do something… he CAN do it! This wipes out *all* excuses for not serving Christ and cease to damage the body which God has given you: including:
>
> - *I cannot quit smoking and drinking.*
>   If God convicted you about destroying your body and life with alcohol, or even drugs, He can give you the power and will to conquer those habits. *What? know ye not that your body is the temple of the Holy Ghost which is in you, which ye have of God, and ye are not your own?* (I Corinthians 6:19)
>
> - *I do not have the time to study my Bible, pray, and go to church.*
>   You can and will, if you let God prioritize your time. *All scripture is given by inspiration of God, and is profitable for doctrine, for reproof, for correction, for instruction in righteousness* (II Timothy 3:16)
>
> - *I cannot live the way a Christian should live because I'll lose all my friends.*
>   Well, God will give you new friends. It is a lie from Hell that Christians have no close friends and cannot have fun.

- *I cannot tell the truth all the time, or I will get in trouble!*
  Maybe forced honesty will steer you away from tempting situations in the first place.

- *I cannot tithe because I barely have enough money to live on every month*
  God can make a *little* go a long way, if you will trust Him! *But my God shall supply all your need according to his riches in glory by Christ Jesus* (Philippians 4:19)

- *I cannot tell others how to be saved because I'm shy; and I don't know what to say.*
  Just try and you will be surprised. God will give you the words; and if you do make mistakes, He will direct you to be more prepared and authoritative. *... take no thought how or what ye shall speak: for it shall be given you in that same hour what ye shall speak* (Matthew 10:19).

All of our excuses are not sufficient to keep us from obeying God. We can do all God requires of us. He will not require of a Christian something that he is not able to do. Jesus told His Apostles not to worry about what they may need to say or how they would say it.

[19] *But when they deliver you up, take no thought how or what ye shall speak: for it shall be given you in that same hour what ye shall speak.*
[20] *For it is not ye that speak, but the Spirit of your Father which speaks in you*   Matthew 10: 19-20

[16] *This I say then: Walk in the Spirit, and ye shall not fulfill the lust of the flesh.*
[17] *For the flesh lusts against the Spirit, and the Spirit against the flesh: and these are contrary the one to the other: so that ye cannot do the things that ye would*   Galatians 5: 16-17

Man is born with a sin nature which has been inherited from Adam. The flesh is always at war with the spiritual man, and is particularly vulnerable to those things which are sinful. This is how Satan has designed his system of lies, deception and things which violate the laws of God. People who reject God and Jesus Christ are called carnal by the apostle Paul. They cannot understand or socially tolerate a true Christian. They are like children with no concept of direction or purpose, like leaves tossed to and fro; carried away with every wind of fleshly pleasure, deceived by men and women with no moral fiber or conscience. The *flesh lusts against the Spirit, and the Spirit against the flesh: and these are contrary the one to the other.*

The force within a Born-again Christian by which the war between flesh and spirit is won by the spirit is the *Holy Spirit*. No man is completely free from sin, no matter how strong the mental conviction of sinful behavior. The war between Satan and all men is *spiritual*, and requires spiritual warfare. The Holy Spirit is the force which will convict each Christian of sin.

[7] Nevertheless I tell you the truth; It is expedient for you that I go away: for if I go not away, the Comforter will not come unto you; but if I depart, I will send him unto you.
[8] And when he is come, he will reprove the world of sin, and of righteousness, and of judgment:
[9] Of sin, because they believe not on me   John 16: 7-9

The Holy Spirit permanently resides in everyone who has been born again, and imparts two things into every true believer: (1) *Gifts* of the Holy Spirit and (2) *Fruits* of the Holy Spirit.

***Gifts* of the Holy Spirit**
In the Old Testament, both the manifestation of the Holy Spirit and selected Gifts of the Holy Spirit were directly by God. Under the New Covenant the Holy Spirit and Gifts of the Holy Spirit are given o every Born-again believer when that person believes by faith in Jesus Christ and surrenders their will and life to Christ. Paul was chosen by God to reveal that under the New Covenant, salvation had come to Jews and

Gentiles alike by faith and grace. Paul was sent to the Gentiles (Galatians 1: 15-16), and the 12 apostles were sent to the Jews led by Peter (Matthew 10: 5-6). Paul was perhaps the most influential missionary who ever lived, and he wrote 13 Books (epistles) in the New Testament which told people how to receive salvation and live in Christ. Paul wrote a great deal about the role of the Holy Spirit in the life of a New Covenant Christian. In his first letter to the Christians in Corinth, he expanded upon the word of Isaiah in the Old Testament concerning gifts from God through and by the Holy Spirit. Paul identified 9 gifts which the Holy Spirit can activate. There are 6 *Power Gifts* and 3 *General Gifts*. Recall that the Holy Spirit under the New Covenant was much more active than the Spirit of God (Holy Spirit) in the Old Testament. In addition to wisdom and knowledge, the Holy Spirit is given to live in every Born-again believer and to strengthen his/her faith. Through faith, a Born-again Christian can exercise the gifts of healing, prophecy, and speaking in tongues (languages). The same true believer who is gifted to speak in a foreign language, might also be given the gift of interpretation of foreign languages so that all who hear might also understand. In both the Old and New Testaments, the group of anointed linguists and scholars who translated Holy Scriptures into either Latin or English attempted to distinguish the *Spirit of God* (upper case) from other *spirits* (lower case). The translators of the King James Bible did a good job in being accurate and consistent, but one should always be able to discern the difference with the help of the Holy Spirit. In I Corinthians 12: 1-10, Paul listed 9 Gifts which are available to Born-again believers through the Holy Spirit.

General Gifts

(1) *The Gift of **Faith***

Faith is the cornerstone of all Holy Spirit Gifts. Faith is what saves you, and it is by faith that we are Born-again. Once a person is Born-again, then God sends the Holy Spirit to dwell in each true believer, and the Holy Spirit will distribute the 6 gifts of supernatural power to each individual as they are called to win souls to Christ.

(2) *The Gift of **Wisdom***

What is wisdom? A secular definition of *wisdom* is: *Wisdom is the use of one's knowledge and experience to make good judgements. It is a rare ability to constantly seek the best way to accomplish a task.* A biblical definition of wisdom is different in both application and outcome. The wisdom which God wants all Christians to possess is wisdom that comes only from God. The wisdom of God (*sapience*) is the use of God's word, spiritual insight, understanding and experience to use good judgement in all things.

*For to one is given by the Spirit the word of **wisdom**; to another the word of knowledge by the same Spirit*
I Corinthians 12:8

True wisdom which reflects the will of God can only come through maturity and the Holy Spirit. True wisdom cannot be found in a sinful world, but only in the love and grace of the Father. Wisdom is not a simple concept, but there are several verses in the Holy Scriptures which address true wisdom.

But the wisdom that is from above is first pure, then peaceable, gentle, and easy to be intreated, full of mercy and good fruits, without partiality, and without hypocrisy   James 3:17

But we speak the wisdom of God in a mystery, even the hidden wisdom, which God ordained before the world unto our glory   I Corinthians 2:7

But we speak the wisdom of God in a mystery, even the hidden wisdom, which God ordained before the world unto our glory   James 1:5

But the wisdom that is from above is first pure, then peaceable, gentle, and easy to be intreated, full of mercy and good fruits, without partiality, and without hypocrisy   James 3:17

To gain wisdom, we must ask God for it (James 1:5), and He will send us true wisdom through the Holy Spirit. Wisdom and knowledge share many similarities. However, the Bible defines wisdom differently from knowledge. Knowledge involves intelligence, while wisdom is deeper than that. It involves understanding and discernment.

(3.0)   *The Gift of **Knowledge***

Knowledge is understanding gained through learning or experience. It can come from secular sources such as a newspaper, television or books, but this type of knowledge is often counter to true spiritual understanding which is built upon wisdom. Human knowledge which is acquired apart from God, is flawed. The Bible refers to knowledge which does not come from God as worthless because it is not usually underpinned by love. (I Corinthians 13:2). *Knowledge puffs up, but love builds up* (I Corinthians 8:1). The pursuit of knowledge for its own sake, without seeking God, is foolishness.

Worldly knowledge is a false knowledge which is opposed to the truth, and Paul urges us to: *Turn away from godless chatter and the opposing ideas of what is falsely called knowledge, which some have professed and in so doing have wandered from the faith* (I Timothy 6:20-21). Human knowledge is opposed to God's knowledge and therefore is no knowledge at all; rather, it is foolishness.

Power Gifts

(1) *The Gift of **Healing***

Medical doctors carry out a mission of physical restoration, and whether admitted or not they are all chosen and given skills by God to heal His people. Christians believe that God can supernaturally heal His people by and through those who have been anointed by the Holy Spirit to heal. This is called *faith healing* and is a special gift to certain mature Christians. Being healed by faith and prayer is a powerful external phenomenon which is spiritual and real. Christians from all denominations have reported that blind see, lame walk and cancer has been healed by prayer and faith. Not everyone is healed, only those who believe in a miracle that is fully within God's will. Both are necessary for restoration. Faith Healing can have a powerful spiritual impact on both those who God chooses to heal and those who observe. James wrote:

[14] *Is any sick among you? let him call for the elders of the church; and let them pray over him, anointing him with oil in the name of the Lord:*
[15] *And the prayer of faith shall save the sick, and the Lord shall raise him up; and if he have committed sins, they shall be forgiven him.*
[16] *Confess your faults one to another, and pray one*

for another, that ye may be healed. The effectual fervent prayer of a righteous man avails much
James 5: 14-16

(2) The Gift of Performing **Miracles**

Jesus Christ performed many miracles during His 3.5 years of ministry. He turned water into wine; He walked on water; and He raised the dead. The Apostle John said that if all of the things which Christ did were written down, there would not be enough books to describe them. *And there are also many other things which Jesus did, the which, if they should be written every one, I suppose that even the world itself could not contain the books that should be written* (John 21:25). Notice what Christ said to His apostles when He personally filled them with the Holy Spirit and sent them throughout the known world. *Verily, verily, I say unto you, He that believeth on me, the works that I do shall he do also; and greater works than these shall he do; because I go unto my Father* (John 14:12). This should be wonderful news to all Born-again believers.

(3 and 4) *The Gifts of* **Speaking in Tongues** *and* **Interpreting Tongues**

In modern Christian circles today, one of the most controversial and divisive topics which is discussed and debated is speaking in tongues. The most vocal church denomination on this issue is the Pentecostal Church. It is generally believed that speaking in tongues became part of Pentecostal theology in 1906. At a revival on Azusa Street in Los Angeles, California, evangelist William J. Seymour preached about baptism of the Holy Spirit and the gift of speaking in tongues. This event seemed to spawn the

Pentecostal movement in which speaking in tongues was adopted as part of salvation by mainstream Pentecostals. The following statements by the late Dr. John F. Walvoord of Dallas Theological Seminary are acknowledged and reflect the beliefs of both authors of this book.

Although speaking in tongues has been a controversial doctrine in the church today, it should be obvious in Scripture that tongues did not occupy a leading role in the activity and worship of the early church. Even though Paul claimed to have spoken in tongues, there is no instance where he used this as a method of preaching the gospel.

Whether or not one believes in tongues as a special spiritual language, the Scriptures are clear that there are certain regulations that govern the use of this gift. In I Corinthians 14, several principles are laid down: (1) Tongues were declared to be the least of the gifts and inferior to *strengthening, encouragement, and comfort* (I Corinthians 14: 1-12). In this connection, Paul made the statement that five words of understanding were more important than ten thousand words in a tongue that is not understood (I Corinthians 14:19). (2) Tongues were to be used in the assembly only when the person speaking could interpret what was said (I Corinthians 14: 13-20). (3) Tongues were intended to be a sign to unbelievers and not to believers (I Corinthian 14:22) (4) Speaking in tongues was to be regulated, and only two or three were permitted to speak in any one service, and then only if an interpreter was present (1 Corinthians 14: 26-38). Unless someone is present to interpret tongues in a church service today, there should be no public speaking in tongues. (5) In a church assembly women were not to speak as a prophet or in tongues (I Corinthian 14:34-35). On the one hand, during the apostolic period Paul recognized the validity of speaking in tongues; on the other hand, speaking in tongues during a church service was forbidden without interpretation. Tongues without interpretation edify no one.

In summary, speaking in tongues is the least of the gifts; it is not a test of salvation but it is one of the 9 spiritual gifts and it is not an indication of spirituality or being saved. These observations are supported by the scriptural record concerning the use of tongues in the early church. The number and type of gifts to everyone is determined by God based upon maturity and service assignments and awarded to each believer by the Holy Spirit. According to Paul, speaking in different kinds tongues is one of the gifts of the Spirit, but he says it is only given to selected believers:

[4] *Now there are **diversities of gifts, but the same Spirit**.*
[5] *And there are differences of administrations, but the same Lord.*
[6] *And there are diversities of operations, but it is the same God which worketh all in all.*
[7] *But the manifestation of the Spirit is given to every man to profit withal.*
[8] *For to one is given by the Spirit the word of wisdom; to another the word of knowledge by the same Spirit;*
[9] *To another faith by the same Spirit; to another the gifts of healing by the same Spirit;*
[10] *To another the working of miracles; to another prophecy; to another discerning of spirits; to another divers kinds of tongues; to another the interpretation of tongues:*

[11] *But all these worketh that one and the selfsame Spirit, **dividing to every man severally as he will***   I Corinthians 12: 3-11

    (5) *The Gift of **Prophecy***

Paul verified the Gift of Prophecy in His letter to the Romans.

Having then gifts differing according to the grace that is given to us, whether prophecy, let us prophesy according to the proportion of faith   Romans 12:6

Paul writes that prophecy is a gift from the Holy Spirit, and that the ability to prophesy is directly proportional to one's faith in Jesus Christ. The Greek work translated as *prophecy* is προφητεύω and it means to *speak or sing by divine inspiration.* The gift of prophecy is, unfortunately, usually equated to foretelling the future. This is undoubtedly true, but the broader meaning of the Greek word for prophecy includes both teachers and preachers.

No one should teach or preach without divine inspiration of scriptural truth. This is why teachers of the word are held more accountable for interpretation of the Holy Scriptures. Deacons and Elders in the church are also held to higher standards than the general congregation (I Timothy 3: 1-16)

Not many of you should become teachers, my brothers, for you know that we who teach will be judged with greater strictness.   James 3.1 (ESV)

Paul had a high regard for those who prophesy, but if the prophesy is spoken in tongues there must be an interpreter.

[1] Follow after charity, and desire spiritual gifts, but rather that ye may prophesy.
[2] For he that speaks in an unknown tongue speak not unto men, but unto God: for no man understands him; howbeit in the spirit he speaks mysteries.
[3] But he that prophesies speaks unto men to edification, and exhortation, and comfort.
[4] He that speaks in an unknown tongue edifies himself; but he that prophesies edifies the church.
[5] I would that ye all spoke with tongues, but rather that ye prophesied: for greater is he that prophesies than he that speaks with tongues, except he interpret, that the church may receive edifying   I Corinthians 14: 1-5

(6) *The Gift of* **Discerning Spirits**

> The average Christian is familiar with the concept of hearing from God. Most Christians will eagerly relate a personal experience that consisted of a dream, vision or some sort of communication by which *God was speaking to them.* What most Christians fail to recognize is that there is another supernatural experience which is that of being contacted or hearing from *Satan.* In the early church and even today there was and still is a real need to distinguish between spiritual communication which came from God through the Holy Spirit, or from Satan. Satan is a master of deception, and he is the father of lies. During the early stages of Christianity, a person would be anointed by the Holy Spirit to distinguish between truth and false teaching. Paul spoke of such an anointing in his letter to both Timothy and Titus in the church at Ephesus.

[3] As I besought thee to abide still at Ephesus, when I went into Macedonia, that thou might charge some that

they teach no other doctrine,
[4] Neither give heed to fables and endless genealogies, which minister questions, rather than godly edifying which is in faith: so do.
[5] Now the end of the commandment is charity out of a pure heart, and of a good conscience, and of faith unfeigned:
[6] From which some having swerved have turned aside unto vain jangling;
[7] Desiring to be teachers of the law; understanding neither what they say, nor whereof they affirm.
I Timothy 1: 3-7

We call these last 6 gifts of the Holy Spirit *power gifts* because the acts of healing, miracles, prophecy, discerning of spirits, speaking in tongues and interpreting tongues can only happen by divine power and with the help of the Holy Spirit. Faith is the *foundation of all the other 6 gifts*, for without faith in the existence of the Father, the Son, and the Holy Spirit, manifestation of all the other gifts is not possible. It is believed that none of the 6 gifts that Paul lists can be exercised without faith. A person cannot be Born-again without faith in Jesus Christ… His work on the cross…and his resurrection from the dead. Once anyone, Jew or Gentile, genuinely accepts Jesus Christ as their Lord and Savior they are instantly Born-again and will receive the Holy Spirit from God. When this happens, that person dies to the world, is transformed into a new creature in Jesus Christ and will begin a spirit filled ministry.

The gifts of the Holy Spirit are necessary to: (1) Carry out the ministry of Jesus Christ until He returns (2) Follow the will of the Father (3) Love others as Christ loved us (4) Edify Christ and (5) Live a victorious Christian life. There are at least 7 Holy Spirit gifts of *power* which can be used to effectively carry out the Ministry of Jesus Christ in His absence. Paul spoke of these gifts of the in his letter to the church at Corinth.

*[9] To another **faith** by the same Spirit; to another the gifts of **healing** by the same Spirit;*
*[10] To another the working of **miracles**; to another **prophecy**; to another **discerning of spirits**; to another **divers kinds of tongues**; to another the **interpretation of tongues**:*
[11] But all these worketh that one and the selfsame Spirit, dividing to every man severally as he will.
[12] For as the body is one, and hath many members, and all the members of that one body, being many, are one body: so also is Christ.
[13] For by one Spirit are we all baptized into one body, whether we be Jews or Gentiles, whether we be bond or free; and have been all made to drink into one Spirit   I Corinthians 12: 9-13

The work that a Born-again Christian will be assigned depends in large part upon how many gifts are activated in the life of that believer. As previously discussed, it is not likely that any one person will exercise and use *all* the gifts, but only those which God assigns to that true believer by the Holy Spirit. An active, effective, and spirit-filled New Covenant church will be composed of members who collectively exercise all the gifts.

[28] And God hath set some in the church, first apostles, secondarily prophets, thirdly teachers, after that miracles, then gifts of healings, helps, governments, diversities of tongues.
[29] Are all apostles? are all prophets? are all teachers? are all workers of miracles?
[30] Have all the gifts of healing? do all speak with tongues? do all interpret?
[31] But covet earnestly the best gifts: and yet shew I unto you a more excellent way   I Corinthians 12: 28-31
*[8] For by **grace** are ye saved through **faith**; and that not of yourselves: it is the **gift of God**:*
[9] Not of works, lest any man should boast.
[10] For we are his workmanship, created in Christ Jesus unto good

works, which God hath before ordained that we should walk in them
Ephesians 2: 8-10

I can do all things through Christ which strengthens me
Philippians 4:13

[4] *For as we have many members in one body, and all members have not the same office:*
[5] *So we, being many, are one body in Christ, and every one; members one of another.*
[6] *Having then gifts differing according to the grace that is given to us*
Romans 12: 4-6

Saul of Tarsus (Paul) was chosen by Jesus Christ on the Road to Damascus to define the New Covenant, establish that salvation would be offered to both Jews and Gentiles, and testify as to the correct way that all New Covenant Christians should live under the New Covenant. There are some who will teach and maintain that spiritual healing, prophecy and miracles no longer exist in the body of Christ. They claim these things ceased with the death of Jesus Christ and His apostles. We wonder how these false teachers dismiss what the Apostle Paul taught in I Corinthians 12: 28-31?

Using the Gifts
The 9 gifts of the Holy Spirit are not available to everyone who says that *I am a Christian*. The Gifts of the Holy Spirit are distributed to each individual when that person is Born-again. Just stop and think about what all 9 of these gifts from the Holy Spirit really accomplish. They represent God Almighty descending upon every true believer in the form of the 3rd person of the Godhead when they accept His Son as their Lord and Savior. God becomes a part of every new believer through the Holy Spirit, and manifests Himself through these 9 gifts. The activation and manifestation of one or more gifts of the Holy Spirit is not automatic. They should be earnestly sought by every Born-again Christian.

[14] ***Neglect not the gift that is in thee****, which was given thee by prophecy, with the laying on of the hands of the presbytery.*
[15] ***Meditate upon these things****; give thyself wholly to them; that thy profiting may appear to all.*
[16] ***Take heed unto thyself, and unto the doctrine****; continue in them: for in doing this thou shalt both save thyself, and them that hear thee*
II Timothy 4: 14-16

This is another *mystery* which is difficult to comprehend. The Holy Spirit has been sent by God at the request of Jesus Christ to dwell inside of every true believer (John 14: 26). The first thing that happens to any individual who has been *spiritually* born-again is that he/she becomes a new creature in Jesus Christ.

Therefore, if any man be in Christ, he is a new creature: old things are passed away; behold, all things are become new   II Corinthians 5:17

When one becomes a *new creature in Christ*, the old passes away and all things are made new in Jesus Christ. That person becomes a part of Jesus Christ and is heir to all of the promises. This miraculous change is not physical but *Spiritual*. The apostle Paul tells us that all believers have died with Christ and no longer live for themselves. Our lives are no longer worldly and physical, but they are now led by the spirit. Our *death* is that of the old sin nature which was nailed to the cross with Christ. It was buried with Him, and just as He was raised up by the Father, so are we raised up to *walk in newness of life*.

[3] *Know ye not, that so many of us as were baptized into Jesus Christ were baptized into his death?*
[4] *Therefore we are buried with him by baptism into death: that like as Christ was raised up from the dead by the glory of the Father, even so we also should **walk in newness of life.***
[5] *For if we have been planted together in the likeness of his death, we shall be also in the likeness of his resurrection:*
[6] *Knowing this, that our old man is crucified with him, that the body of*

sin might be destroyed, that henceforth we should not serve sin
Romans 6: 3-6

The new person that will be raised up is what Paul refers to in II Corinthians 5:17 as a *new creation*. The Holy Spirit is the *Agent* or vehicle through which a new believer is baptized into Jesus Christ.

Therefore, if any man be in Christ, he is a new creature: old things are passed away; behold, all things are become new   II Corinthians 5:17

This is not the baptism of the Old Covenant or John's baptism of repentance; but a new supernatural, *Spiritual* birth. Part of that Spiritual transformation is to receive forgiveness of all sin and become a New Adam……. The Old Adam has passed away. That is why Paul said:

What? know ye not that your body is the temple of the Holy Ghost which is in you, which ye have of God, and ye are not your own?
I Corinthians 6:19

[22] *For as in Adam all die, even so in Christ shall all be made alive.*
[45] *And so it is written: The first man Adam was made a living soul; the last Adam was made a quickening Spirit*
I Corinthians 15: 22, 45

Once this new creature in Christ accepts and activates the gifts which God gives them by the Holy Spirit, this new life in Christ manifests itself through the *Fruits of the Spirit*.

Fruits of The Holy Spirit
The fruits of the Holy Spirit are those things that
can only be found in a Born-Again Christian who is accept and use the gifts that God gave them. Recall that there are 9 Fruits of the Holy Spirit (Galatians 5: 22-23). A world of unbelievers seeks to find these 9 gifts, but they cannot be found. Only a Christian who is sure that he/she will be saved by Jesus Christ and is assured of eternal life can ever achieve

its state of existence. One who can go through life joined to Jesus Christ can truly find the Kingdom of God here on earth, for these things are what will be found in eternal life in a new, sinless world. This what Matthew meant when he declared.

*From that time Jesus began to preach, and to say: Repent: for the **Kingdom of Heaven** is at hand* Matthew 4:17

We are to place all of our cares, our woes and misery upon Him. He wants us to come to Him as little children and believe that only He is *the way, the truth, and the life.*

[16] *This I say then, Walk in the Spirit, and ye shall not fulfill the lust of the flesh.*
[17] *For the flesh lusts against the Spirit, and the Spirit against the flesh: and these are contrary the one to the other: so that ye cannot do the things that ye would.*
[18] *But if ye be led of the Spirit, ye are not under the law.*
[19] *Now the works of the flesh are manifest, which are these; Adultery, fornication, uncleanness, lasciviousness,*
[20] *Idolatry, witchcraft, hatred, variance, emulations, wrath, strife, seditions, heresies,*
[21] *Enviers, murders, drunkenness, retellings, and such like: of the which I tell you before, as I have also told you in time past, that they which do such things shall not inherit the Kingdom of God.*
[22] **But the fruit of the Spirit is love, joy, peace, longsuffering, gentleness, goodness, faith,**
[23] **Meekness, temperance**: *against such there is no law.*
[24] *And they that are Christ's have crucified the flesh with the*

affections and lusts.
[25] *If we live in the Spirit, let us also walk in the Spirit*
Galatians 5: 16-25

Diversity of Gifts: *Old Testament vs New Testament*
It is seldom mentioned and perhaps not even recognized that there is a significant difference between the Gifts which were given to man by God under the Old Covenant, and those given to man at the request of Jesus Christ, by God the Father, through the Holy Spirit (John 14: 15-18). The following graphic dramatically contrasts the difference.

Both Old Testament men of faith and New Testament Christians worship the same God, and he is omnipotent, omnipresent, and omniscient; so why would there be a difference in number and content? There are two obvious reasons. *First*, in the Old Testament, there was no plan of salvation that needed to be spoken to all the people throughout the known world. Salvation was offered only to the Jews. There was no need to raise up apostles of God who would preach to both Jews and

Gentiles concerning salvation. *Second,* all Jews lived under the Laws of Moses (given to Moses by God), and salvation under the law was simple… obey the law, serve God, and *live*. Violate the law (any part of the law) and *die* (physically and spiritually). This period of history was known as the *Dispensation of the Law*, and only those that died with the *Faith of Abraham* believed that God would one day send a redeemer to forgive their sins. This is in dramatic contrast to the *Dispensation of Faith,* in which any person (Jew or Gentile) can be saved by accepting Jesus Christ as their Lord and Savior. Under the New Covenant, the Holy Spirit was sent to dwell in each Born-again Christian, and bring with Him the Gifts of the Holy Spirit. These are actually not *gifts of the Holy Spirit*, but they are *gifts from God* to accomplish His eternal purpose. Note that fundamentally the Gifts which God gave to selected individuals in the Old Testament enabled those who operated in the gifts to deal with social, societal, and physical problems. In the New Testament, both the evidence and impact of the gifts are more spiritual in power and use.

Summary

The Holy Spirit cannot be found in every person. It is a gift that is only given to every Christian who is born again and has been crucified with Christ. The Bible declares that the Holy Spirit is *the power of God* (II Timothy 1:7); that it *leads us to all truth* (John 14:17, 26); it enables us to *discern Spiritual things* (I Corinthians 2:11, 14); it is our *guarantee (seal) of eternal life* (Ephesians 1:13-14); and that *without* it we are *not His* (Romans 8:9). Perhaps the most important thing that the Holy Spirit does for every born-again Christian is to baptize every true believer into Jesus Christ. The baptism of the Holy Spirit may be defined as that work whereby the Spirit of God places the believer into union with Christ and into union with other believers in the body of Christ This is a Spiritual transformation by which every true believer becomes a part of the body of Christ. As a member of the Body of Christ, one becomes an heir and joint heir to all promises. The apostle John said:

I knew him not: but he that sent me to baptize with water, the same said unto me: Upon whom thou shalt see the Spirit descending, and remaining on him, the same is he which baptizes with the Holy Ghost. John 1:33

We were all baptized by one Spirit into one body   I Corinthians 12:13
For John truly baptized with water; but ye shall be baptized with the Holy Ghost not many days hence   Acts 1:5

Know ye not, that so many of us as were baptized into Jesus Christ were baptized into his death?   Romans 6:3

The Holy Spirit is that spiritual vehicle by which every true believer can join the body of Christ and enter in communion with God the Father. Without the indwelling of the Holy Spirit, the spirit man cannot communicate with God the spiritual man. God is a spirit, and spiritual things cannot understand or communicate with non-spiritual things. We communicate with God by prayer and faith. He lives within us as **through His word and the Holy Spirit within us**. The Holy Spirit helps us understand His word and His will; and apply it to our lives.

[9] *But ye are not in the flesh, but in the Spirit, if so be that the Spirit of God dwell in you. Now if any man has not the Spirit of Christ, he is none of his.*
[10] *And if Christ be in you, the body is dead because of sin; but the Spirit is life because of righteousness.*
[11] *But if the Spirit of him that raised up Jesus from the dead dwell in you, he that raised up Christ from the dead shall also quicken your mortal bodies by his Spirit that dwelleth in you.*
[12] *Therefore, brethren, we are debtors, not to the flesh, to live after the flesh.*
[13] *For if ye live after the flesh, ye shall die: but if ye through the Spirit do mortify the deeds of the body, ye shall live.*
[14] *For as many as are led by the Spirit of God, they are the sons of God.*   Romans 8: 9-14

In the Garden of Eden, God and Adam communicated in a personal way, not through any intermediatory. Before the Law was given to Moses and the people of Israel, communication was face to face as two men normally talk, or in dreams or visions. Adam and Eve would hear from God only when God chose to commune and communicate with man. Under the Old Covenant and the Law, common man was separated from God and could only be heard through the High Priest and Moses, or on special occasions when God or the Holy spirit came to man for special assignments and purpose. Under the New Covenant, communication with God is enabled by the Holy Spirit through prayer and faith. When the Church Age ends; God the Father will once again communicate with God directly through His Son Jesus Christ for 1000 years in the Millennial Kingdom. Jesus Christ will rule over the entire world just outside the New Jerusalem on His Throne of Glory, which will sit in a New Holy Temple on a great elevated plateau.

The eternal plan of God will finally be realized after the earth is purged of all sin and the eternal Kingdom of God begins. At that time, God's Great Plan for the redemption of all mankind will be completed, and God will once again commune with Man just as He did with Adam and Eve before sin entered the world and Paradise was Lost.

Chapter 4
Evidence of the Holy Spirit

The Holy Bible in the New Testament has much to say about the role of the Holy Spirit in a Born-again believer's life. Any Christian will recognize the rightful place of the Holy Spirit as a member of the eternal triad of God the Father, Jesus Christ the Son, and the Holy Spirit. Few Christians can summarize the remarkable role that the Holy Spirit plays in a Born-again believer's spiritual life.

Gift of the Holy Spirit

The *gift* of the Holy Spirit should not be confused with the *gifts* of the Holy Spirit. The scriptures contain many references to the *Gift of the Holy Spirit*. That gift *proceeds* from God and is given to all who would believe upon His son Jesus Christ and are Born-again.

If ye then, being evil, know how to give good gifts unto your children: how much more shall your heavenly Father give the Holy Spirit to them that ask him?   Luke 11:13

The gift of eternal life is by faith and grace. It is an eternal, free gift to all who would be Born-again. However, there is another gift which comes at the moment of salvation. It is called the *Holy Spirit*. The Holy spirit cannot be bought, and it cannot be earned by works. When one decides in *faith* to die to this world and become a servant to our Lord Jesus Christ, salvation comes by *grace* from our Lord and Savior Jesus Christ and His Father. The Holy Spirit is sent to dwell in every Born-again Christian as a guarantee. This transformation from death to life… light to darkness… lost to the world and hidden in Christ… is the most important moment in anyone's short life on this earth. Christ was speaking to a group of Publicans and sinners; He was admonished for talking to sinners and eating with them. In response He said:

I tell you, there is joy in the presence of the angels of God over one sinner who repents   Luke 15:10

Salvation is a gift from God by faith, but it is received by each individual as a free-will decision. This principle can be found throughout scripture. Adam and Eve sinned in the Garden of Eden and never received the Holy Spirit within them because it was their free will to do so. Noah and his family were saved from the great flood because they chose to build an ark when it had never even rained. Judas betrayed Jesus Crist because he chose to do so for 30 pieces of silver.

God does not pick and choose who will be saved, that decision is made by each individual. He does not want anyone to be cast into the Lake of Burning Fire, but wants all to enter into eternal life (II Peter 3:9; II Timothy 2:4-6) with him and His Father. Jesus died for the sins of every person (I John 2:2) and He *predestined* that all will be saved. Unfortunately, not everyone will accept the free gift of expiation in our Lord and Savior, Jesus Christ. Those who would answer the call will be saved by faith, and they will be glorified in Jesus Christ.

[28] *And we know that all things work together for good to them that love God, to them who are the called according to his purpose.*
[29] *For whom he did foreknow, he also did predestinate to be conformed to the image of his Son, that he might be the firstborn among many brethren.*
[30] *Moreover whom he did predestinate, them he also called: and*

whom he called, them he also justified: and whom he justified, them he also glorified   Romans 8: 28-30

The concept of *predestination* has perhaps caused more confusion and disbelief in those who seek to understand God than any other principle in the Holy Scriptures. The rationale is that since God has predestined those who will be saved, then why worry about it? A person is either saved or not saved by divine choice. This can only be explained by the full council of scripture and the parallel concept of free-will. God has had a plan to redeem mankind ever since Adam and Eve sinned and lost their relationship with a sinless God. Since time began, God foreknew that Adam and Eve would sin and that through the seed of Adam all men would have a desire to sin and rebel against God. God did not originally *plan* that Adam and Eve would disobey His commands. He told Adam and Eve to populate the earth and if they obeyed His only law (Genesis 1: 1-3) they would live and commune with Him forever. God *predestined* this for Adam and His progeny, but they willfully rejected His purpose and plan. In the fullness of time, God would send His Son Jesus Christ into the world to die on the Cross of Calvary for the sins of the entire world…past, present, and future. Salvation and eternal life would then be offered by faith and grace to all who would believe.

He that believeth on the Son hath everlasting life: and he that believeth not the Son shall not see life; but the wrath of God abideth on him.   **John 3:36**

It seems clear that God does not pick and choose who will be saved. He doesn't want anyone to perish (II Peter 3:9; II Timothy 2: 4-6). Jesus died for the sins of *every* person (I John 2:2). Any theology or line of reasoning that leads to God choosing who will be saved and who will not be saved is not taught anywhere in the Word of God. God has predestined that *all* can spend eternity in a state of love, peace, and joy; but sadly not all will do so. The Holy Scriptures are quite clear on this issue: *Not everyone that saith unto me, Lord, Lord, shall enter into the kingdom of heaven; but he that doeth the will of my Father which is in heaven* (Matthew 7:21). It is the Gift of the Holy Spirit that seals our promises of the Father.

In whom ye also trusted, after that ye heard the word of truth, the gospel of your salvation: in whom also after that ye believed, ye were sealed with that Holy Spirit of promise   Ephesians 1:13

Wherefore I give you to understand, that no man speaking by the Spirit of God calleth Jesus accursed: and that no man can say that Jesus is the Lord, but by the Holy Ghost   I Corinthians 12:3

It is clear from the words of Paul that not only is the Holy Spirit a special gift from God to accomplish His eternal plans, but the Holy Spirit speaks to the Father and confirms to Him that Jesus Christ is your Lord and Savior. The Holy Spirit is a witness that you have been redeemed from the curse of sin, chosen to leave a world of sin in spirit and in truth, and now lives to serve Christ. That is why Jesus said:

[22] *Many will say to me in that day, Lord, Lord, have we not prophesied in thy name? and in thy name have cast out devils? and in thy name done many wonderful works?*

[23] *And then will I profess unto them, I never knew you: depart from me, ye that work iniquity*   Matthew 7: 22-23

How God reveals Himself to a Born-again believer by the Holy Spirit was different in the Old Testament than in the New Testament. In the Old Testament it was to give to only selected individuals a revelation of His glory and sovereignty (Ezekiel 28:22). The Holy Spirit (Spirit of God) was given to accomplish His eternal purpose and plan. Under the New Covenant, it is a permanent gift to *all* Born-again believers.

The Holy Spirit can be revealed in many ways. We will broadly categorize the *presence* of the Holy Spirit in 4 ways:

      (1) *Manifestation* of the Holy Spirit
      (2) *Indwelling* of the Holy Spirit
      (3) *Infilling* of the Holy Spirit
      (4) *Conviction* by the Holy Spirit

Manifestation of The Holy Spirit

[7] But the manifestation of the Spirit is given to every man to profit withal.
[8] For to one is given by the Spirit the word of wisdom; to another the word of knowledge by the same Spirit;
[9] To another faith by the same Spirit; to another the gifts of healing by the same Spirit;
[10] To another the working of miracles; to another prophecy; to another discerning of spirits; to another different kinds of tongues; to another the interpretation of tongues:
[11] **But all these worketh that one and the selfsame Spirit,** *dividing to every man severally as he will*   I Corinthians 12: 7-11

The first thing that happens to any individual who has been spiritually born-again is that he/she becomes a new creature in Jesus Christ. The old passes away, and all things are made new in Jesus Christ. That person becomes a part of Jesus Christ and is heir to all of the promises. This is called a *baptism* by the Holy Spirit.

The Holy Spirit baptizes a new Born-again Christian into Christ. The set of all believers is called the *body of Christ*.

*Now ye are the **body of Christ**, and members in particular*
I Corinthians 12:27
*For as the **body** is one, and hath many members, and all the members of that one **body**, being many, are one **body**: so also is Christ*
I Corinthians 12:12

Once a Born-again Christian becomes a new creature in Christ, the Holy Spirit is sent to dwell in that individual. The Holy Spirit then activates different Gifts of the Holy Spirit as God directs Him to do so. Selected gifts from God through His Holy Spirit are granted to each individual to carry out the work of the ministry. The power to use these gifts is also through the Holy Spirit. This new life in Christ manifests itself through service, and that individual is rewarded the *Fruits of the Spirit*.

The Holy Spirit *proceeds* from the Father.

*But when the Comforter is come, whom I will send unto you from the Father, even the **Spirit of truth, which proceedeth from the Father**, he shall testify of me* John 15:26

The Holy Spirit is a member of the heavenly Godhead: God the Father, God the Son, and God the Holy Spirit. The Holy Spirit is a living part of God the Father, but beyond that embodiment of God, little can be comprehended as to its origin and appearance. It is seldom recognized, but according to John, Jesus Christ also proceeded from God.

*Jesus said unto them, If God were your Father, ye would love me: for **I proceeded forth and came from God**; neither came I of myself, but he sent me* John 8:42

The content of John 8:42 and John 15:26 is remarkable! The implication and impact are directly to the concept of a *Holy Trinity*. The doctrine of the Trinity teaches that only one God exists. Within the nature of this one God, there are three distinct persons or centers of consciousness. There is a false view of the Trinity known as *Tritheism*. There are some religions which hold Tritheism as a core belief that the Father, Son and Holy Spirit exist as three complete gods who are independent and self-existing. Tritheism rejects the idea of one God or the unity of God but teach that God the Father, Jesus Christ, and the Holy Spirit are three separate persons and each are full gods. Tritheism is neither taught in the Holy Bible nor has it been the historic belief of the church. It is an incorrect way of explaining the nature of God. Comparing John 8:42 to John 15:26 should destroy the belief that Tritheism is scriptural.

God is a spirit and Holy. The Apostle John is unique in identifying the Holy Spirit as the *paraclete*. The term *paraclete* is only found in the Johannian texts and appears five times: John 14:16, John 14:26, John 15:26, John 16:7, and I John 2:1. The word has a complex meaning and is a combination of the Greek words *para* (being with someone) and *kalein* (to call out or assign). Paraclete is translated as *counselor* in the Revised Standard Version and *comforter* in King James Version).

[16] *And I will pray the Father, and he shall give you another Comforter, that he may abide with you forever;*
[17] *Even the Spirit of Truth; whom the world cannot receive, because it sees him not, neither knoweth him: but ye know him; for he dwelleth with you, and shall be in you.*
[18] *I will not leave you comfortless: I will come to you*
John 14: 16-18

These words of Jesus as recorded by the Apostle John are short but rich with content. *First*, the Holy Spirit was promised to His disciples (and all Born-again believers) as a *Comforter,* and will abide with all true believers forever. *Second*, the Spirit of Truth (Holy Spirit) will dwell within every Born-again and will be a source of authority and truth. *Third*, Jesus Christ will not leave His chosen disciples *comfortless* (Greek word ὀρφανός …. *bereaved* or *desolate*). The Holy Spirit is also mentioned in Ephesians 1: 13-14 where believers are said to be *sealed* with the Holy Spirit.

[13] *In whom ye also trusted, after that ye heard the word of truth, the gospel of your salvation: in whom also after that ye believed, ye were sealed with that holy Spirit of promise,*
[14] *Which is the earnest of our inheritance until the redemption of the purchased possession, unto the praise of his glory*   Ephesians 1: 13-14

The concept of being sealed with the Holy Spirit is one of ownership and possession. God has promised eternal life to all who believe in Christ, and as a guarantee that He will keep His word, He has sent the Holy Spirit to indwell the believer until the day of redemption (II Corinthians 1:22, Ephesians 4:30).

***Indwelling* of the Holy Spirit**
I will pray the Father, and he shall give you another Comforter, that he may abide with you forever
John 14:16

And we are his witnesses of these things; and so is also the Holy Ghost, whom God hath given to them that obey him   Acts 5:32

The apostles at the Lord's Last Supper were told (John 14:26) by Jesus

Christ that the Holy Spirit would come in His name, and help them remember all that He had spoken to them and The Holy Spirit would teach them all things.

But the Comforter, which is the Holy Ghost, whom the Father will send in my name, he shall teach you all things, and bring all things to your remembrance, whatsoever I have said unto you   John 14:26

This happened to His apostles and disciples on the Day of Pentecost Today, the Holy Spirit is given to all Born-again Christians at the moment of true surrender to Jesus Christ. God is manifested in your life through the Holy Spirit. The Holy Spirit cannot be obtained by good works, and it cannot be obtained by prayers, supplication, and request. Once a person believes by faith in Jesus Christ, and decides to follow His commandments, that person begins a spiritual transformation by which he/she is said to be *Born-again*. At that moment God will *seal* your commitment by sending the *Holy Spirit* to dwell within that person.

*Marvel not that I said unto thee, Ye must be **born again***   John 3:7

*In whom ye also trusted, after that ye heard the word of truth, the gospel of your salvation: in whom also after that ye believed, ye were **seal**ed with that holy Spirit of promise*   Ephesians 1:13

*Know ye not that **ye are the temple** of God, and that the Spirit of God dwelleth in you?*   I Corinthians 3:16

The manifestation of the Holy Spirit produces the change that instantly takes place when anyone is Born-again. The first act of the Holy Spirit is to baptize that new believer into the body of Christ. This is in stark contrast to what took place on the Day of Pentecost. The Holy Spirit fell upon 3000 Jewish converts with *fire*, and was given to each Jew that was there in Jerusalem by the risen Jesus Christ Himself. This was a fulfillment of what John the Baptist prophesied at the baptism of Jesus when He began His 3.5-year ministry of reconciliation and redemption.

John answered, saying unto them all, I indeed baptize you with water; but one mightier than I cometh, the latchet of whose shoes I am not worthy to unloose: **he shall baptize you with the Holy Ghost and with fire**   Luke 3:16

At the Feast of Pentecost there were 3000 Jews who believed upon Jesus Christ, and at that moment they were all received Holy Spirit, but the Holy Spirit was given to each true believer by Jesus Christ. Pentecost was a Jewish Feast; Jesus lived and died as a Jew; and salvation was offered to the Jews first.

For I am not ashamed of the gospel of Christ: for it is the power of God unto salvation to everyone that believeth; to the Jew first; and also to the Greek   Romans 1:16

Paul had not yet revealed the *Mystery* of the New Covenant: Salvation would be offered to both Jews and Gentiles by faith and grace.

Under the New Covenant revealed by the Apostle Paul, a person instantaneously receives God's gift of the Holy Spirit the moment he is born again. This means that today, in the Age of Faith and Grace, the manifestations of the Holy Spirit are available only to those Christians who have personally yielded their life to Jesus Christ. Unfortunately, there are many so called Christians who will never experience the joy, power and indwelling of the Holy Spirit because they have not been Born-again. Church pews are full of good, decent, and sincere people who have been deceived into thinking that they are saved and redeemed: But they are not. It is not enough to attend church every Sunday, sing songs of praise and contribute to the offering plate as it is passed. How sad. *No one* can see the Kingdom of Heaven unless they have received the Holy Spirit (John 3:5, I Corinthians 12:3, Romans 8:13, Ephesians, II Thessalonians 2:13, Romans 8:11). No Holy Spirit, no *new birth*. No Holy Spirit, no *direct spiritual communication with God the Father*. No Holy Spirit, no *victory over sin*. No Holy Spirit, no *progress in sanctification.* No Holy Spirit, no *spiritual wisdom.* No Holy Spirit, no *spiritual gifts.* No Spiritual Gifts, no *Fruits of the Spiritual Gifts.*

> *Question:* Can a person be saved without receiving the Holy Spirit?
> *Answer:* No

A person cannot be saved without the Holy Spirit. You cannot grow as a Christian, and enter a personal relationship with Jesus without the Holy Spirit. The Holy Spirit convicts us of sin, He leads us into all truth, He lives in us to be our advocate, and He seals us for salvation.
We must reluctantly, and with prayer and conviction, conclude again that there are many Christians who live their whole lives in the church, think that they are saved… but are not. This is because they have not completely given their life to Jesus Christ, received the Holy Spirit, and been baptized into the Body of Christ.

[8] So then they that are in the flesh cannot please God.
*[9] But ye are not in the flesh, but in the **Spirit**, if so be that the **Spirit** of God dwell in you. Now if any man have not the **Spirit** of Christ, he is none of his.*
*[10] And if Christ be in you, the body is dead because of sin; but the **Spirit** is life because of righteousness.*
*[11] But if the **Spirit** of him that raised up Jesus from the dead dwell in you, he that raised up Christ from the dead shall also quicken your mortal bodies **by his Spirit that dwelleth in you**.*
[12] Therefore, brethren, we are debtors, not to the flesh, to live after the flesh.
*[13] For if ye live after the flesh, ye shall die: but if ye through the **Spirit** do mortify the deeds of the body, ye shall live.*
*[14] For as many as are led by the **Spirit** of God, they are the sons of God*   Romans 8: 8-14

After a person receives the Holy Spirit, he/she dies to the world and is made alive in Jesus Christ. We are baptized into the Body of Christ, and begin our journey as a new creature in Jesus Christ. We learn to yield to the Holy Spirit in our thoughts, feelings, and actions. As we mature and grow, we see God's glory and goodness poured out on our lives because we are learning how to live for God and obey the commands of His Son, Jesus Christ. There is a great desire which wells up within us to read and study the Holy Scriptures. The words of God bring life and new meaning to our daily lives. The old man which was born of Adam gradually becomes the new man in Jesus Christ. Be assured that the world will not understand this transformation, and those who live in sin without considering the final payment for sin will reject you and your new life.

For the wages of sin is death; but the gift of God is eternal life through Jesus Christ our Lord   Romans 6:23

Be not deceived; God is not mocked: for whatsoever a man soweth, that shall he also reap   Galatians 6:7

[11] *In whom also we have obtained an inheritance, being predestinated according to the purpose of him who worketh all things after the counsel of his own will:*
[12] *That we should be to the praise of his glory, who first trusted in Christ.*
[13] *In whom ye also trusted, after that ye heard the word of truth, the gospel of your salvation:* **in whom also after that ye believed, ye were sealed with that Holy Spirit of promise,**
[14] **Which is the earnest of our inheritance** *until the redemption of the purchased possession, unto the praise of his glory*   Ephesians 1: 11-14

When one is Born-again and receives the Holy Spirit: *What gifts does one receive?* The Holy Spirit is given by God at the request of Jesus Christ. God is complete and holy in all things, and when the Holy Spirit proceeds from God it has *all* of the gifts of the Holy Spirit. Every gift that could be granted to a true believer is present and available.

The indwelling of the Holy Spirit is often called the *baptism* of the Holy Spirit. The term is found in the Gospel of Luke and in the Book of Acts. Paul wrote in his letter to the church at Corinth:

[12] For as the body is one, and hath many members, and all the members of that one body, being many, are one body: so also is Christ.
*[13] **For by one Spirit are we all baptized into one body**, whether we be Jews or Gentiles, whether we be bond or free; and have been all made to drink into one Spirit.*   I Corinthians 12: 12-13

Paul makes it clear that we as Born-again Christians are baptized into the body of Christ. This is what it means to be a Born-again Christian. The Holy Spirit acts and moves in such a way that we are brought to real faith and united spiritually in Jesus. Compare this to what Luke wrote in Acts 1:5.

For John truly baptized with water; but ye shall be baptized with the Holy Ghost not many days hence   Acts 1:5

Luke is affirming what John the Baptist said in Luke 3:16 when he baptized Christ in the River Jordan.

John answered, saying unto them all, I indeed baptize you with water; but one mightier than I cometh, the latchet of whose shoes I am not worthy to unloose: he shall baptize you with the Holy Ghost and with fire   Luke 3:16

Luke confirms that Jesus Christ was baptized in water by John the Baptist, but this was not the baptism that would be accomplished by Jesus Christ at the Feast of Pentecost, or by the Holy Spirit after Paul revealed the Mystery of the New Covenant. John the Baptist baptized Jews in the River Jordan for *repentance* to prepare them for the arrival of Jesus Christ. On the Day of Pentecost, *Christ* baptized only Jews with the Holy Spirit. Under the Old Covenant, the priests all had to immerse themselves in water to be ritually clean, and anyone who would enter the temple for an atoning sacrifice had to be ritually clean by baptism. When our Lord and Savior ascended to heaven after His resurrection, He was *already* sinless and clean. When we are Born-again and receive the Holy Spirit, we become spiritually a part of the sinless and resurrected body of Jesus Christ. When He died on the Cross of Calvary, the veil which separated people in the Holy Place from where God dwelled in the Holy of Holies was rent from top to bottom. The barrier which separated man from God was no longer there. When a person is Born-again, the Holy Spirit allows one to enter into the very presence of God justified. The Holy Spirit baptizes us into the body of Christ, and positionally we are already seated in the heavenlies with our Lord Jesus Christ next to God the Father.

[1] *And you hath he quickened, who were dead in trespasses and sins;*
[2] *Wherein in time past ye walked according to the course of this world, according to the prince of the power of the air, the spirit that now worketh in the children of disobedience:*
[3] *Among whom also we all had our conversation in times past in the lusts of our flesh, fulfilling the desires of the flesh and of the mind; and were by nature the children of wrath, even as others.*
[4] *But God, who is rich in mercy, for his great love wherewith he loved us,*
[5] *Even when we were dead in sins, hath quickened us together with Christ, (by grace ye are saved;)*
[6] *And hath raised us up together, and made us sit together in heavenly places in Christ Jesus*   Ephesians 2: 1-6

This is possible by the *indwelling* of the Holy spirit at the point in time when we are *Born-again*. When the Holy Spirit takes up residence in our mortal body, it brings with it *all* of the Gifts of the Holy Spirit. However, every gift is not automatically active in the Born-again believer's life.

Infilling of the Holy Spirit

The Holy Spirit cannot be bought or summoned by sinful man, and it is a not automatically given to anyone who simply says, *Lord, Lord*. The Holy Spirit can only be obtained 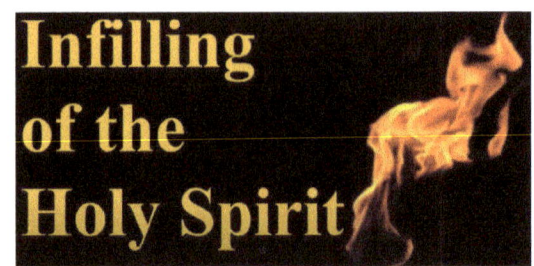 only by those "Christians" who are Born-again. At the moment of surrender (only God knows), the Holy Spirit *proceeds* from God at the request of His Son Jesus Christ, and takes up residence in the spirit part of the three-fold man (Body, Soul and Spirit). The *old man* is crucified, and the *new man* is born spiritually. At that moment, the Holy Spirit resides in the new man.

What? know ye not that your body is the temple of the Holy Ghost which is in you, which ye have of God, and ye are not your own?
I Corinthians 6:19

When the Holy Spirit arrives, He functions not only as our guarantee of eternal life and to seal our relationship with God the Father, but to bring *power* to the new man in Christ.... Power to preach the Gospel, power to live like Jesus taught us to live, and power over Satan who is continuously seeking to devour your faith. The Christian life is impossible to live without the Holy Spirit. There is a constant battle being fought not only between you and Satan, but between your carnal (fleshly) man and your internal (spiritual man). For many, defeat and discouragement characterize their Christian life. The Christian life is impossible to live out of your own strength, God does not want defeat and discouragement to characterize the true believer. To strengthen each true believer, God has provided His Holy Spirit. He has commanded believers to live the Christian life by being filled with the Spirit. The total infilling of a true believer can rarely be achieved. The new person in Christ must grow and mature. As that happens, more and more responsibility and gifts of the Holy Spirit will be made manifest as God commands the Holty spirit to do so. This is generally called *sanctification*, and it is a life-long process.

The Christian who has spiritually experienced the process of being Born-again is not a *baby* Christian, but is also not fully mature in Christ. A Born-again Christian who possesses the Holy Spirit begins a life-long journey to be more like Christ. Any *righteousness* in a true Christian is imputed to that individual by Jesus Christ. Any person who exercises and uses gifts of the Holy Spirit is *empowered* by the Holy Spirit in which the gifts reside. When the Holy Spirit arrives, *every* gift of God is resident in that believer. There is *One God and Father of all, who is above all, and through all, and in you all*. Ephesians 4:6). Romans 12, I Corinthians 12 and Ephesian 6 list multiple gifts of the Holy Spirit. In Ephesians 6 Paul reveals a list of extraordinary gifts which are all given to only a relative few.

[11] *And he gave **some**, apostles; and some, prophets; and some, evangelists; and some, pastors and teachers;*
[12] *For the perfecting of the saints, for the work of the ministry, for the edifying of the body of Christ:*
[13] *Till we all come in the unity of the faith, and of the knowledge of the Son of God, unto a perfect man, unto the measure of the stature of the fulness of Christ*   Ephesians 4: 11-13

In over 60 years of Christian ministry, the authors have never known anyone who exercise all of the gifts. Anyone who dedicates their life to Christ and serves as a pastor will exercise many of the gifts, but usually not all. The life of a Christian is to be more like Jesus Christ and exhibit the Holiness of God. Of course, this is impossible because in spite of our personal relationship with Jesus Christ, we can never fully conform to His image. He was sinless and man is not…He alone is fully righteous and man is not…. He is a spiritual man and we are not. God is the supreme ruler of the universe, and man cannot even comprehend His nature and power. The closest that we might come to conforming to Jesus Christ is to obey His one commandment upon which all the others rest:

[28] And one of the scribes came, and having heard them reasoning together, and perceiving that he had answered them well, asked him, Which is the first commandment of all?
[29] And Jesus answered him, The first of all the commandments is, Hear, O Israel; The Lord our God is one Lord:
[30] And thou shalt love the Lord thy God with all thy heart, and with all thy soul, and with all thy mind, and with all thy strength: this is the first commandment.
[31] And the second is like, namely this, Thou shalt love thy neighbor as thyself. There is none other commandment greater than these.
Mark 12: 28-31

The infilling of the Holy Spirit is that process by which a Born-again Christian lives by the Spirit, growing and maturing in Jesus Christ. The spirit filled Christian will, as time goes by, continually seek the gifts. As one grows, it will become more natural to live a spirit-filled life and follow Jesus Christ. Christ said:

Verily, verily, I say unto you, He that believeth on me, the works that I do shall he do also; and greater works than these shall he do; because I go unto my Father John 14:12

I will not leave you comfortless: I will come to you John 14:18

But the Comforter, which is the Holy Ghost, whom the Father will send in my name, he shall teach you all things, and bring all things to your remembrance, whatsoever I have said unto you John 14:26

What a glorious promise! But there is an even greater promise which will be fulfilled when Christ comes again to claim His bride.

[2] In my Father's house are many mansions: if it were not so, I would have told you. I go to prepare a place for you.
[3] And if I go and prepare a place for you, I will come again, and

receive you unto myself; that where I am, there ye may be also.
[4] And whither I go ye know, and the way ye know John 14: 2-4

[9] But as it is written, Eye hath not seen, nor ear heard, neither have entered into the heart of man, the things which God hath prepared for them that love him.
[10] But God hath revealed them unto us by his Spirit: for the Spirit searches all things, yea, the deep things of God.
[11] For what man knoweth the things of a man, save the spirit of man which is in him? even so the things of God knoweth no man, but the Spirit of God.
[12] Now we have received, not the spirit of the world, but the spirit which is of God; that we might know the things that are freely given to us of God I Corinthians 2: 9-12

Infilling of the Holy Spirit happens when a person is receives the Holy Spirit. Everything that is needed to do the works of Jesus Christ are there to continue the work which Jesus Christ started during his 3,5-year ministry. This spiritual activity is not only a result of maturity and faith in Jesus Christ which will grow as each person strives to be more like Christ and conform to His image, but it appears that a follower of Jesus Christ can experience infilling instantaneously and repeatedly to sustain and strengthen the faith of each spirit-filled Christian.

And they were all filled with the Holy Ghost, and began to speak with other tongues, as the Spirit gave them utterance Acts 2:14

[17] Wherefore be ye not unwise, but understanding what the will of the Lord is.
[18] And be not drunk with wine, wherein is excess; but be filled with the Spirit Ephesians 5:17

When Elizabeth heard Mary's greeting, the baby leaped in her womb; and Elizabeth was filled with the Holy Spirit Luke 1:41

So, Ananias departed and entered the house, and after laying his hands on him said, "Brother Saul, the Lord Jesus, who appeared to you on the road by which you were coming, has sent me so that you may regain your sight and be filled with the Holy Spirit   Act 9:17

And the disciples were continually filled with joy and with the Holy Spirit   Acts 13:52

Conviction by the Holy Spirit
And when he is come, he will reprove the world of sin, and of righteousness, and of judgment   John 16:8

In John 16:8, the word reprove in Greek is *elegchos*, and it means to provide evidence or proof that leads to *conviction* or reproof. In the New Testament, it is associated with the work of the Holy Spirit in convicting individuals of sin and unrighteousness. The world is a sinful place and one task of the Holy Spirit is to convict the world of its sin. No amount of preaching, pleading, or pointing of fingers will bring about the conviction of sin unless the Holy Spirit is at work in the sinner's heart. It is the Spirit's job to convict. What is the most basic sin of which the world is guilty? It is *unbelief*. The world is in a state of rebellion and sin because it does not believe in Jesus Christ.

The sins of the world are manifestations of Satan's prescence and influence in the world. It is not the forgiveness of sins which has already been accomplished by Christ on the Cross of Calvary, it is repentance of sins and sinful acts which will bring each person into a covenant relation with Jesus Christ: This is faith made manifest in redemption. It is the sin of unbelief—a refusal to trust in Jesus—that must be dealt with. Jesus said that the Holy Spirit will convict and redeem anyone who will just believe in faith that He is able to create a new, Born-again Christian in Jesus Christ. How sad it is that anyone would choose to not believe Chrit and follow Satan and his destructive lies. Once a person is convicted by the Holy Spirit, a transformation will take place.

Can One Lose the Holy Spirit?
A popular topic to preach in any Christian church today is the Doctrine of *once saved, always saved*. It is taught in most Christian denominations today that once a person is saved and enters a personal relationship with God, they are secure in His promises, and no matter what happens they are assured of eternal life in the Kingdom of God. We have consistently proposed that salvation is not just saying daily prayers, going to church every Sunday, or believing that Jesus Christ died on the Cross of Calvary. To receive the promises of God and walk in faith, power, and conviction one *MUST BE BORN-AGAIN*. Every person is born in the flesh will sin, die, and deteriorate. Every person is born with a Body, Soul and a Spirit. The Soul is that part of man which will live forever. The Spirit is that part of man which gives life. Every person is born with a spirit of rebellion and sin, which is closely connected and influenced by the heart, mind, and the external body of man. The internal man is connected to the external man by the 5 main senses: *smell, touch, sight, hearing,* and *taste*. The inner man is constantly at war with the outer man, but after being Born-again the Holy Spirit will be your advocate who will strengthen you and convict sin when you are tempted

The Holy Scriptures reveal that the Holy Spirit can be *grieved*. This implies that this is something that can only happen to an individual after He/she has been Born-again. This is confirmed by Paul in Ephesians 4:30.

And grieve not the Holy Spirit of God, whereby ye are sealed unto the day of redemption   Ephesians 4:30

The *Greek word* translated as *grieve* in Ephesians 4:10 is σβέννυμι; which means to *suffer, sorrow, suppress, extinguish,* or *be offended*. This identifies the Holy Spirit as one who can reason, suffer, sorrow and be offended. To grieve the Holy Spirit is only recorded in this verse. Paul follows this warning with a list of things which by association *grieve* the Spirit of God.

[31] *Let all **bitterness**, and **wrath**, and **anger**, and **clamor**, and **evil speaking**, be put away from you, with all malice:*
[32] *And be ye kind* (**lack of kindness**) *one to another, tenderhearted, forgiving (**unforgiveness**) one another, even as God for Christ's sake hath forgiven you.*

Paul writes that it is possible to grieve and torment the Holy Spirit, but this is not the same as losing the Holy Spirit.

In the Old Testament the Holy Ghost (Holy Spirit) could definitely be lost or returned to God from whence it came. The first King of Israel (King Saul) was chosen by the people to rule and reign over them. The people wanted a King like every other nation (I Samuel 8: 19-20) …. How foolish! Samuel and the people chose Saul, and it was a day of great regret. God accepted the will of His people (I Samuel 10:1), and He gave Saul the Spirit of God to help Saul rule wisely and righteously (I Samuel 10:6). However, Saul soon apostatized and became a wicked, Godless, King. *God will not be deceived or mocked* and in His righteous anger he removed the Holy Spirit from Saul (I Samuel 16:14).

Sampson was another casualty of sinful living. Sampson took the *Nazarite vow* to separate themselves for service to God (Numbers 6: 1-21). Samuel and John the Baptist also took the Nazarite vow. The Old Testament clearly states that the Spirit of the Lord was active in Sampson, enabling him to perform heroic feats (Judges 16-30). Sampson attributed his great strength to his uncut hair, but all of his strength and power come from the Lord and the Holy Spirit. A Nazarite could not drink alcoholic beverages, eat fruits of the vine, and could never cut their hair. Sampson was a mighty man of valor and he became a legend of strength and physical strength for the Lord. Sampson was anointed with the Spirit of God on at least 4 different occasions. However, Samson exercised his free will, drank strong wine, and committed forbidden sexual acts with a Philistine woman called Delilah. After a night of drinking and sexual intercourse, Delilah betrayed him and cut his hair. Sampson not only lost his hair, but he also lost his anointing by the Holy Spirit (Judges 16:20). Without divine power, Sampson was blinded in both eyes and chained between two columns in a Philistine temple (Judges 16:25). In a stunning act of redemption, Sampson repented, and by the grace of God was allowed to pull the entire temple down and kill 3000 Philistines. The Spirit of God also came upon Othniel (Judges 3:9-10), Gideon (Judges 6:34) and Epitaph (Judges 11:29)

King David certainly believed that the Holy Spirit was a gift from God for special reasons. David was given the Holy Spirit to serve as the 2nd King of Israel (II Samuel 23: 1-2), but he also fell into apostasy and sin as did Saul before him. But, David *pleased God* because he always did what God instructed him to do (Acts 13:22) and after the flesh betrayed him and he committed a sinful act, he repented. David knew that he had sinned against God, and he was afraid that God would remove his anointing (The Holy Spirit) as he had to King Saul.

Cast me not away from thy presence; and take not thy holy spirit from me Psalms 51:11

Of course, this proves nothing except that the Spirit of God came directly from God in the *Old Testament*, and God could remove it any time He chose to do so. These five incidents all occurred during the *Dispensation of the Law* (Phillips, *The Eternal Plan of God*). We are now in the *Dispensation of Faith and Grace*, and we cannot assume that just because God gave and took back His Holy Spirit in the Old Testament that He would do so in the New Testament. *What can we discern from the Book of Truth in the New Testament?*

In the New Testament, it has already been established that the Holy Spirit is given to a person by God at the moment of being Born Again (John 15:26). It is "good prechin" to assure a Christian that once a person has been Born-again, received the gift of the Holy Spirit, and began a new life in Jesus Christ that salvation and eternal life is *sealed* by the Holy Spirit, and it is permanent. The issue to be addressed does not concern the seal of the Holy Spirit, but the permanency of that seal. This doctrine is called *once saved, always saved*. While some will argue that "once saved, always saved" is a comforting assurance of God's grace at work in your life, others will argue it gives people a free pass to live how they want and think they can still go to heaven. The following passages in scripture *seem to indicate* that once-saved, always saved is sound doctrine.

Who hath also sealed us, and given the earnest of the Spirit in our hearts II Corinthians 1:12

[13] *In whom ye also trusted, after that ye heard the word of truth, the gospel of your salvation: in whom also after that ye believed, ye were **sealed** with that holy Spirit of promise,*
[14] *Which is the earnest of our inheritance until the redemption of the purchased possession, unto the praise of his glory*   Ephesians 1: 13-14

However, carefully examining both I Corinthians 1:12 and Ephesians 1: 13-14, neither actually state that once a person is Born-again, no amount of sinful behavior or negligence can ever cause a loss of the indwelling Holy Spirit. Loss of faith and returning to sinful behavior after being Born-again is called *backsliding*. There is one verse in the New Testament which implies that the Holy Spirit *can* be taken from a Born-again believer, and that salvation and eternal life are only guaranteed to all who never fall away or abandon the faith.

[4] *For **it is impossible** for those who were once enlightened, and have tasted of the heavenly gift, and were made partakers of the Holy Ghost,*
[5] *And have tasted the good word of God, and the powers of the world*

to come,
[6] *If they shall **fall away**, to renew them again unto repentance; seeing **they crucify to themselves the Son of God** afresh, and put him to an open shame*   Hebrews 6: 4-6

Hebrews 6: 4-6 refers to someone who has *tasted of the heavenly gift, and were made partakers of the Holy Ghost*. A major role of the Holy spirit in all Born-again believers is to convict, teach and comfort. We can be sure that anyone who has been Born-again is *not isolated* from sin, and is continuously tempted to sin and destroy their relationship with both Jesus Christ and God. The body is still corrupted and is vulnerable to sin. Even though the inner man is at peace with God, there is a constant war between the flesh and the Holy Spirit. Paul is quite clear that if anyone has tasted of the goodness of living in Christ and has received the promise of the Holy Spirit: *If they shall fall away, to renew them again unto repentance*. That Paul refers to true Christians will be apparent from the following commentary which is largely based upon an opinion written by that great Christian theologian, Albert Barnes (December 1, 1798 - December 24, 1870).

> We will analyze to state the true meaning of this passage by an examination of the words and phrases in detail, observing that it refers to true Christians; that the object is to keep them from apostasy; and that it teaches that if they *should* apostatize, it would be impossible to renew them again or to save them. That it refers to true Christians will be apparent from the following discussion.
>
> *Fall Away...*
> The author of Hebrews is not speaking of the falling away of superficial Christians who have never been Born-again. Such have nothing to fall away from, but an empty faith, or hypocritical profession. Neither is he speaking of partial decline or *temporary backsliders*. The falling away is here used is an open and avowed renouncing of Christ, deliberate and willful continuing acts of sin.

Falling away is a continuous and deliberate effort to return to the ways of the world and sinful behavior after they have received the knowledge of the truth and tasted the goodness of Jesus Christ. It is written that if this is the continual behavior of a Born-again Christian, it is *impossible* to renew them again unto repentance. Not because the blood of Christ is sufficient to obtain pardon for this sin, but this sin in its very nature is opposite to repentance and everything that leads to it. If there are those who misinterpret the truth of this passage, fear that there is no mercy for them if they completely resist Christ and apostatize after experiencing the goodness of God, there is good reason to fear for their souls. We should ourselves beware, and caution others, of every approach near to a gulf so awful as apostasy and retreat into a gulf of sin, yet in doing so we should keep close to the word of God, and be careful not to wound and terrify the weak, or discourage the fallen and penitent. Born-again believers not only taste of the word of God, but they drink it in… they live in it…and they understand the difference in wrath and grace. But, the common, nominal Christian who continues to be a hearer of the word and not a doer; is not only unfruitful but produces nothing but deceit and selfishness. They are near the awful state described by the writer of Hebrews.

For it is impossible….
It should be noted that Hebrews 6:4-6, has for almost 2000 years created much controversy, and that the opinions of commentators, theologians, preachers, and denominational Christians are greatly divided in regard to its meaning. It is suggested that this controversial passage is intended to describe those who were once Born-again Christians… those who have once been awakened and enlightened…. and then choose to purposely sin and fall away from the faith. Others maintain that it refers to those who have professed to be true Christians, have not been Born-again, and received the Holy Spirit, and who then apostatize. Hebrews 6:4 does not seem to suggest this last interpretation.

*For **it is impossible** for those who were once enlightened, and have tasted of the heavenly gift, and were made partakers of the Holy Ghost*   Hebrews 6:4

Most Christians have interpreted Hebrews 6: 4-6 largely based upon what they have heard and not truthful and through exegesis of Holy Scripture. An unbiased examination and interpretation of Hebrews 6: 4-6 will result in the following conclusions.

    (1) Unless each reader of Hebrews 6: 4-6 has some private opinion to defend, the body of Christians who live under the New Testament would consider these verses as describing true Christians.

    (2) The author was warning anyone who had committed to a life in Jesus Christ that if the body is not put into servitude to the spirit, and if that person turns to sin and disobedience to the Laws of God and to the Commands of Jesus Christ; there are serious consequences. The object was to keep those who were awakened and enlightened from apostasy, and preserve those who were already in the church of Jesus Christ from returning to life in the flesh. The object of this warning are those who professed to be a believer and, but who were not truly converted. The author did not say that once a person is converted and saved, they can never fall away. But, these new Christians in Rome were told that they could *not* be renewed again and be saved if they should fall away ….. because they would have rejected the only plan of salvation after they had heard and accepted it, and willingly renounced the grace of God and His eternal plan of redemption after they had tasted its saving power. If God's plan of forgiveness of sin by the crucifixion of Jesus Christ and salvation by faith and grace could not save them… what could?

How shall we escape the wrath of God, if we neglect so great a salvation, by what other means could they be brought to God?
Hebrews 2:3

For if we sin willfully after that we have received the knowledge of the truth, there remains no more sacrifice for sins
 Hebrews 10:26

This interpretation of Hebrews 6: 4-6 support the exact meaning of the phrases which the author uses. A careful and honest examination of this text will reveal that the writer refers to those who are sincere believers. The phrase *it is impossible* obviously and properly denotes absolute impossibility. It has been contended, by Storr and others, that it denotes only great difficulty. But the meaning which would at first strike all readers would be that *the thing could not be done*; that it was not merely very difficult, but impossible. The Greek word ἀδύνατον which is translated *impossible* occurs only in Matthew, Mark, Luke, and the Book of Hebrews. In each case, it denotes that the thing could not be done: (Matthew 19:26; Mark 10:27). Luke writes: *the things which are impossible* (ἀδύνατον) *with men are possible with God* (Luke 18:27). Hebrews 6:18 says: *In which it was impossible* (ἀδύνατον) *for God to lie* and *Without faith it is impossible* (ἀδύνατον) *to please God* (Hebrews 11:6). Every usage of ἀδύνατον denotes absolute impossibility.

They crucify themselves....
These passages show that it is not merely a great difficulty to which the apostle refers, but that it is *impossible* and could not be done. If this is the correct interpretation of Hebrews 6: 4-6, then it proves that if those referred to should fall away, they could never be renewed…. their case was hopeless, and they must perish. If a Born-again Christian should apostatize, or fall from grace: *He never could be renewed again* and could not be saved.

Paul did not teach that he might fall away and be renewed again as often as he pleased. He had other views of the grace of God than this; and he meant to teach that if a man should ever abandon

Christ for the sins of the world, his case was hopeless… and he will perish.

Enlightened ….
For those who were once enlightened: The phrase "to be enlightened" is one that is often used in the Scriptures, and may be applied either to one whose understanding has been enlightened to discern his duty, though he is not converted, or more commonly to one who is truly converted (Ephesians 1:18). It does not of necessity refer to true Christians, though it cannot be denied that it suggests the idea that the heart is truly changed, and that it is more commonly used in that sense (Psalm 19:8).

Light……
Light in the scriptures is a type of knowledge, holiness, and happiness, and there is no impropriety here in understanding it in accordance with the more decisive phrases which follow, as referring to true Christians. Christ said that *He is the light which shines in the darkness, and that He is the light of the world.*

And have tasted ……
To *taste* in the Scriptures means to *experience* or to *understand*. The expression is derived from the fact that *taste* is one of the means by which we ascertain the nature or quality of an object; compare (Matthew 16:28; John 8:51; Hebrews 2:9). The concept is that those being addressed here have *experienced* the heavenly gift.

The heavenly gift ….
The gift which did not come from man, but from heaven. The expression means some favor or gift which has given from God, and includes those gifts conferred upon man by the Holy Spirit. It also includes the plan of salvation and the forgiveness of sins. The use of the article **the** heavenly gift limits it to something special. It is an expression which is directed to sincere Christians. By construction and use, it certainly applies to the gift of the Holy

Spirit. Holy Spirit. It is only in this context that we can partake of the Holy Spirit. We "partake" of food when we share it with others; we "partake" of pleasure when we enjoy it with others; we "partake" of spoils in war when they are divided between us and others. So, we partake of the power and gifts of the Holy Spirit when we share them with other people... saved or unsaved.

Although it is true that an unpardoned sinner may be enlightened and awakened by the Holy Spirit, the scope and context of Hebrews 6: 4-6 cannot be directed at an unbeliever. Noted scholars such as Grotius, Bloomfield, and others, understood this passage to primarily refer to the miraculous gifts of the Holy Spirit.

Summary
Considering the full council of scripture, it has been stated that the Holy Spirit will not be given to anyone until they have had a complete and life-changing experience of being Born-again. It is difficult to ignore the clear and inspired words of Hebrews 6: 4-6. If one has tasted (experienced) the gift of the Holy Spirit and the impact of that transformation.... and then decides to turn away from both the commands of Jesus Christ and the power of the Holy Spirit... then the Holy Spirit *cannot* continue to dwell in that individual. The conclusion and result of that falling away from the truth and the light of Jesus Christ is that it is impossible to experience being Born-again and repentance to good works if one rejects the spiritual rebirth which is part of being Born-again. It must be clear that this decision to apostatize and reject the Holy Spirit and the Grace of God is a decision that was made by *him or her* that has fallen from grace. It is the ultimate result of how Satan and a sinful world can overcome faith and salvation when man lives in the world and not in Jesus Christ.

Chapter 5

Live and Be Led by the Spirit

The Holy Spirit is sent by God to dwell in every Born-again believer at the moment that one decides to live a life in Jesus Christ, and leave a world of sin for a life clothed in the righteousness of Christ. This is called being *Born-again.* The importance of such a decision cannot be overemphasized, and it has been proposed that this is not just a decision that is a part of Christian belief and faith, but it is a spiritual transformation that *must* take place to inherit the Kingdom of God. This is not just conjecture, Christ said that: *You must be Born-again.* This command of Jesus Christ has been the underlying theme of this entire book.

Jesus Christ is the only person born sinless by a supernatural birth whose conception came from the Holy Spirit and Mother Mary, and He then lived a sinless life for 33.5 years. When he died, Jesus Christ offered His pure, sinless life as a permanent atonement for sin. Jesus Christ fulfilled His destiny by never saying or doing anything unless God the Father told Him to do so. In other words, Christ surrendered His life to the Father and lived within His Holiness.

Even if it were possible for anyone to live a sinless life, the original sin would condemn him to *death* because the wages of sin…any sin…is death. This being the truth: *How can man ever expect to stand before*

God justified? The answer is profound and yet so simple that anyone can understand.

Justification

The 3.5-year ministry of Jesus Christ ended when Christ died for the sins of the world on the Cross of Calvary. Under the Old Covenant, salvation could only be attained by works and obeying the Law, which no man could ever do. Disobeying the Laws of God was sin, and the wages of sin is death (Romans 6:23). Only Jesus Christ was born without sin, and then lived a sinless life. Because He was sinless, He and He alone could offer Himself as the pure and perfect sacrificial Lamb of God. He took upon Himself the sins of the entire world... Past, Present and Future... and offered Himself as the final and complete sacrifice for Sin. Before the death of Jesus Christ, no man could stand before God without being condemned because of sin. The work of Jesus Christ in forgiving the sins of the world is called *Justification*.

Justification by Christ was *unilateral*, and required no action or agreement by sinful man. The atoning sacrifice of Jesus Christ settled the Sin issue, but it did not save anyone. In order to attain *salvation* and escape eternal punishment in the Lake of Burning fire, any Jew or Gentile must be saved by faith. Faith that Jesus Christ is the Son of God, died for the sins of the world, was resurrected from the Grave after 3 days and 3 nights, and now sits on the right-hand-side of God the Father.

Sanctification

Sanctification is the process of being set apart for God's special purpose and growing in holiness. It involves a transformation that makes a believer more like Jesus Christ over time, which consists of both an initial act of being made holy through faith in Jesus Christ, surrendering to His will, and a continual growth in holiness throughout a believer's life. It is an ongoing process by which a believer seeks to be more lake Christ. It emphasizes the importance of living according to God's truth and commands, as each Born-again believer is called to become more like Christ over time.

The Process of Sanctification will not be completed until each Born-again Christian is Judged at the Bema Seat Judgment. Final judgment by God is not based upon sin, but is completely determined by faith. The only way that sinful man can stand before God the Father and then be *glorified* is to join his mortal, sin ridden body with the perfect, sinless body of Jesus Christ. *Justification* is a gift from God which was fully accomplished by Jesus Christ on the Cross of Calvary: *Sanctification* begins when a Christian is Born-again, and it is a life-long journey which will not be completed until the final judgment.

Glorification

Glorification is the transformation of sinful man into a new, sinless spiritual man with a new glorified and incorruptible body which will be clothed in Robes of Righteousness; pure and white. The appropriation of salvation is by the Grace of God. Glorification and can only be attained by faith, and is appropriated by the Grace of God. This is clearly a *spiritual* transformation which will only be attained after the rapture of the saints. It is the final cleansing of all sin from both our inner man and the outer man. When Christ returns in the air to gather all of His *ecclesia* to Him (living and dead), we will be awarded a new sinless, incorruptible body (I Corinthians 15:57), and we will be clothed in white robes of righteousness (Revelation 7:9). At the last trumpet, when Jesus comes, the saints will undergo a fundamental, instant transformation… the *perishable* will put on the *imperishable* and the *corruptible* will become *incorruptible*.

[51] Behold, I shew you a mystery; We shall not all sleep, but we shall all be changed,
[52] In a moment, in the twinkling of an eye, at the last trump: for the trumpet shall sound, and the dead shall be raised incorruptible, and **we shall be changed.**
[53] For this corruptible must put on incorruption, and this mortal must put on immortality.
[54] So when this corruptible shall have put on incorruption, and this

mortal shall have put on immortality, then shall be brought to pass the saying that is written, Death is swallowed up in victory.

When a person is Born-again, God… at the request of His Son Jesus Christ… sends the Holy Spirit as a guarantee of permanent *Justification*, *Sanctification* and *Glorification*.

Righteousness

Any *righteousness* that a person might attain in this journey is *imputed* from Jesus Christ and will not be completed until every Born-again believer stands before the throne of God, receives a new incorruptible body and is clothed in robes of white.

When a person is Born-again, a miracle that only God can accomplish takes place. When Jesus Christ, the Son of God, died on the Cross of Calvary; it was His own choice to fulfill the wishes of His Father in heaven. Christ could have called upon a legion of angels to remove His beaten and battered body from the Cross at any Time. Christ could have died in His fleshly body as any other man, and ascended to heaven sinless by virtue of His sinless life. He chose to bear the sins of the world on His sinless self, and He died to please the Father and redeem sinful man.

Praise God Forever !!!!

[1] *My little children, these things write I unto you, that ye sin not. And if any man sin, we have an advocate with the Father, Jesus Christ the righteous:*
[2] *And he is the propitiation for our sins: and not for ours only, but also for the sins of the whole world.*
[3] *And hereby we do know that we know him, if we keep his commandments.*
[4] *He that saith, I know him, and does not keep not his commandments,*

is a liar, and the truth is not in him.
[5] But whosoever keeps his word, in him verily is the love of God perfected: hereby know we that we are in him.
[6] He that saith he abides in him ought himself also to walk, even as He walked   I John 2: 1-6

Born-again: A New Creature in Jesus Christ

John made it crystal clear that Christ died for our sins…yours and mine. When one is Born-again, He allows us to enter into a new, spiritual bond with Him and inherit part of His righteousness. We become a *new creature* in Jesus Christ and we are transformed into the light of His glory and leave the darkness of Satan and sin. This is a *spiritual* transformation, but it is must be recognized that this is also a *physical transformation*.

When one is Born-again, that person dies to the word and is made alive in Jesus Christ. We become a member of the body of Christ, and that *new man* is fully committed to living for Christ and serving Him. *How can this be?* It is impossible without the Holy Spirit to help us, sustain us, empower us and lead us in our new life. When one is *Born-again*, the Holy spirit is sent to live within our Spiritual Man and is our *paraclete*. The Holy spirit comes to live within us and is our *guarantee* that we can live a new life in Christ. He is our advocate, spiritual advisor and a source of power from God.

*[3] Blessed be the God and Father of our **Lord Jesus Christ**, who hath **blessed us with all spiritual blessings** in heavenly places in Christ:*
*[4] According as he hath chosen us in him before the foundation of the world, that **we should be holy** and without blame before him in love:*
[5] Having predestinated us unto the adoption of children by Jesus Christ to himself, according to the good pleasure of his will,
*[6] To the praise of the glory of his grace, wherein **he hath made us***

accepted in the beloved.

*[7] In whom **we have redemption through his blood**, the **forgiveness of sins**, according to the riches of his grace;*

*[8] Wherein **he hath abounded toward us in all wisdom and prudence**;*

[9] Having made known unto us the mystery of his will, according to his good pleasure which he hath purposed in himself:

*[10] That in the dispensation of the fulness of times **he might gather together in one all things in Christ**, both which are in heaven, and which are on earth; even in him:*

*[11] In whom also **we have obtained an inheritance**, being predestinated according to the purpose of him who worketh all things after the counsel of his own will*   Ephesians 1: 3-11

This is the glorious result of being Born-again, and the Holy Spirit is given to each true believer who surrenders his life to serve Jesus Christ and dies to the world. This newness of life in our Lord Jesus Christ… even though we still live in a sinful body… is called *Walking in the Spirit.*

Walking in the Spirit

*There is therefore now no condemnation to them which are in Christ Jesus, who **walk** not after the flesh, but after the Spirit*   Romans 8:1

*This I say then: **Walk** in the Spirit, and ye shall not fulfill the lust of the flesh*   Galatians 5:16

*[16] Know ye not that ye are the **temple** of God, and that the Spirit of God dwelleth in you?*
*[17] If any man defile the **temple** of God, him shall God destroy; for the **temple** of God is holy, which **temple** ye are*   I Corinthians 3: 16-17

The *first* step in walking in the Spirit (Holy Spirit) is to be Born-again and receive the Gift of the Holy Spirit. The *second* step is to trust and listen to the Holy Spirit who will lead you in all things.

Howbeit when he, the Spirit of truth, is come, he will guide you into all truth: for he shall not speak of himself; but whatsoever he shall hear, that shall he speak: and he will shew you things to come   John 16:13

These words should comfort you, strengthen you and assure you that it is possible to live a new life in Jesus Christ. There are some principles which should be observed as you serve Christ as a *new man*, a *second Adam*.

[24] *...they that are Christ's have crucified the flesh with the affections and lusts* (of the flesh)
[25] *If we live in the Spirit, let us also* **walk** *in the Spirit*
Galatians 5: 24-25
[26] *Likewise the Spirit also helps our infirmities: for we know not what we should pray for as we ought: but the Spirit itself maketh intercession for us with groanings which cannot be uttered.*
[27] *And he that searches the hearts knoweth what is the mind of the Spirit, because he maketh intercession for the saints according to the will of God*   Romans 8: 26-27

The Holy spirit will *intercede* for you. Do not confuse Walking in the Spirit with Gifts of the Spirit which were discussed in Chapter 3. When the Holy Spirit intercedes for you; obey what He will tell you in faith. You must turn to the Holy spirit for daily guidance on how to walk in Christ. Jesus called the Holy Spirit the *Spirit of Truth*. Jesus assured us that:

[13] *Howbeit when he, the* **Spirit of Truth**, *is come, he will guide you into all truth: for he shall not speak of himself; but whatsoever he shall hear, that shall he speak: and he will shew you things to come.*
[14] *He shall glorify me: for he shall receive of mine, and shall shew it unto you*   John 16: 13-14

*[16] This I say then: **Walk in the Spirit**, and ye shall not fulfill the lust of the flesh.*
[17] For the flesh lusts against the Spirit, and the Spirit against the flesh: and these are contrary the one to the other: so that ye cannot do the things that ye would   Galatians 5: 16-17

The *Spirit of Truth* is like an inner compass in our lives … always pointing us toward what Jesus would say or do in any given moment. When we respond; we walk in the Spirit.

Praying in the Spirit
God is a spirit and we are flesh and blood. If any Born-again Christian is to talk to God, it must be in a spiritual language. *How can one pray in the spirit?* When one receives the Gift of the Holy Spirit, one also receives the tongues of angels or a spiritual prayer language (I Corinthians 13:1). This is not the Gift of Tongues; it is a spiritual prayer language which is spoken between God and the Holy Spirit. When you need help (and you will), ask the Holy Spirit to give you *strength, wisdom,* and *Power*. These are Gifts of the Holy Spirit, but they come from God. In order to be an effective witness for Jesus Christ, you *must* rely upon the Holy Spirit.

Living in the Spirit
[15] If ye love me, keep my commandments.
[16] And I will pray the Father, and he shall give you another Comforter, that he may abide with you forever;
[17] Even the Spirit of truth; whom the world cannot receive, because the world sees him not, neither knows him: But ye know him; for he dwells with you, and shall be in you.
[18] I will not leave you comfortless: I will come to you.
John 14: 15-17

One of the primary roles of the Holy Spirit is to constantly sustain you and support you as to live in the Spirit. To live in the Spirit is actually a misnomer, because the Holy Spirit is simply responding to the commands, desires, and instructions of God the Father. The Holy Spirit *proceeds* from God and is the spiritual gateway to the constant presence of God in our daily lives.

Howbeit, when he, the Spirit of truth, is come, he will guide you into all truth: for he shall not speak of himself; but whatsoever he shall hear, that shall he speak: and he will shew you things to come   John 16:13

Part of the mystical process of being born again is for the new creature in Jesus Christ to begin a journey of spiritual maturity in which we seek to be conformed to His image and be like Him. This is a life-long journey and although the Holy Spirit will guide us, help us, and give us instructions from God the Father: No Christian can ever walk toward that goal without the Holy Spirit.

For now, we see through a glass, darkly; but then face to face: now I know in part; but then shall I know even as also I am known
I Corinthians 13:12

But we all, with open face beholding as in a glass the glory of the Lord, are changed into the same image from glory to glory, even as by the Spirit of the Lord   II Corinthians 3:18

In his epistle to the Galatians, Paul admonished those Christians there to not only *live* in the spirit but *walk* in the spirit.

[11] But I certify you, brethren, that the gospel which was preached of me is not after man.
[12] For I neither received it of man, neither was I taught it, but by the revelation of Jesus Christ   Galatians 1: 11-12

If we live in the Spirit, let us also walk in the Spirit   Galatians 5:25

Paul constantly walked in the spirit and spread the gospel primarily to the Gentiles, speaking only what had previously been revealed to him by the risen Christ. Jesus Christ revealed that He never said anything or did anything that God did not tell Him to do. We also receive our commands and instructions from Jesus Christ through God and the Holy Spirit.

Witnessing in the Spirit
The Spirit itself bears witness with our spirit, that we are the children of God Romans 8:16

There are many Christians who say that they cannot witness for Christ because they do not know what to do, what to say, or how to say it. This is a common lie that Satan will put in the mind of every Christian. A Born-again Christian need not worry that they are not articulate enough or bold enough to witness for Christ. These are excuses from Satan to block a sincere desire to serve Christ. There age several things beside witnessing which are required to edify Christ and are needed to support the ministry: *I will bring donuts each Sunday and serve coffee* or *I can greet people at the door of the church. I can serve as an usher every Sunday*. Certainly, these things are part of church and religious services and they are fully appreciated and make people feel wanted; but they are only secondary to the real purpose: *Winning Souls to Jesus Christ*. We can identify at least 7 things that Jesus taught His apostles and His disciples in preparation for their world-wide ministry. We should also heed His words.

1. He sent each Apostle or disciple to a particular place where the Gospel message was needed to bring hopeless sinners into a personal relationship with Jesus Christ (Acts 13:2)
2. Jesus had personally taught the Word and the plan of salvation to those He sent into the world (Luke 10: 1-24)
3. Jesus instructed them to only speak what the Father told them to speak, and do only what God had instructed them to do (John 15:5)
4. Jesus had personally anointed them with power and authority to spread the Word
5. The Word of Truth would speak for them and provide all the authority needed to convert Jews to follow Jesus Christ, and reveal

the plan of salvation to the Gentiles for the first time (Ephesians 6: 10-11)
6. Jesus told them: But when they deliver you up, take no thought of how or what ye shall *speak*: for it shall be given you in that same hour what ye shall *speak.* Do not worry about what you shall say, how you will live or where your power will come from (Matthew 10:19)

[2] *And he sent them to preach the kingdom of God, and to heal the sick.*
[3] *And he said unto them: Take nothing for your journey, neither staves, nor scrip, neither bread, neither money; neither have two coats apiece*   Luke 9: 2-3

These instructions from Christ to His Apostles and His disciples are just as valid today as they were 2000 years ago. Christ is still leading us, teaching us, and filling us full of His power and authority as we go to unbelievers today. The only difference is that Christ has sent to every Born-again Christian the Holy Spirit, who will instruct us and lead us, speaking only what Jesus Christ and God the Father wants us to hear. The Holy Spirit will not only tell us what to do, but lead us in all things. Jesus taught and spoke directly to His apostles and disciples. Those who are led by the Spirit will always be dependent on spiritual, supernatural power: That is why Jesus sends the Holy Spirit to live in every Born-again believer. Jesus fully expected those He sent forth to become spiritually *mature disciples* who would then make *more disciples*. This is one of the primary functions of every pastor who stands and teaches in a pulpit today.

Being Led by the Spirit
[14] *For as many as are led by the Spirit of God, they are the sons of God.*
[15] *For ye have not received the spirit of bondage again to fear; but ye have received the Spirit of adoption, whereby we cry, Abba, Father.*
[16] *The Spirit itself bears witness with our spirit, that we are the*

children of God:
[17] *And if children, then heirs; heirs of God, and joint-heirs with Christ; if so be that we suffer with him, that we may be also glorified together* Romans 8: 14-17

What a glorious promise! The world is full of lonely, dejected, friendless, and forsaken people. Every Born-again Christian is *never alone*, either spiritually or physically.
   ...I will never leave thee, nor forsake thee   Hebrews 13:5

It is a lie from Satan that a Christian can never have any fun, is constantly rejected by society, and has no place to go but Church. The world will reject you and abandon you for serving Christ, but a true Christian will never desert you, because their entire existence and ministry hangs upon one word: *love*.

[34] *A new commandment I give unto you: That ye love one another; as I have loved you, that ye also love one another.*
[35] *By this shall all men know that ye are my disciples, if ye have love one to another*   John 13: 34-35

The following is an excerpt from *The MacArthur New Testament Commentary* on Galatians 5.

> [17] *For the flesh lusts against the Spirit, and the Spirit against the flesh: and these are contrary the one to the other: so that ye cannot do the things that ye would.*
> [18] *But if ye be led of the Spirit, ye are not under the law.*
> Galatians 5: 17–18
>
> Along with many other verses in the New Testament, Galatians 5: 17-18 make it obvious that walking by the Spirit is not simply a matter of passive surrender. The Spirit-led life is a life of conflict, because it is in constant combat with the old ways of the

flesh that continue to tempt and seduce the believer. The flesh sets its desire against the Spirit, and the Spirit against the flesh.

A believer who is not actively involved in resisting evil, and seeks to follow Christ without the Holy Spirit is not being led by the Spirit. The Born-again Christian is a *good soldier of Christ Jesus* who is engaged in the *active service* of his Lord (II Timothy 2: 24-26).

To be *led by the Spirit* is the same as *walking in the Spirit*. The two go hand in hand, but walking in the Spirit carries additional emphasis on His leadership. We do not walk along with Him as an equal, but follow His leading as our sovereign, divine Guide.

For all who are being led by the Spirit of God, these are sons of God
Romans 8:14

The converse is also true: Those who are sons of God are led by the Spirit of God. Believers do not need to pray for the Spirit to lead, because He is already doing that. They need to seek willingness and obedience to follow Him to victory.

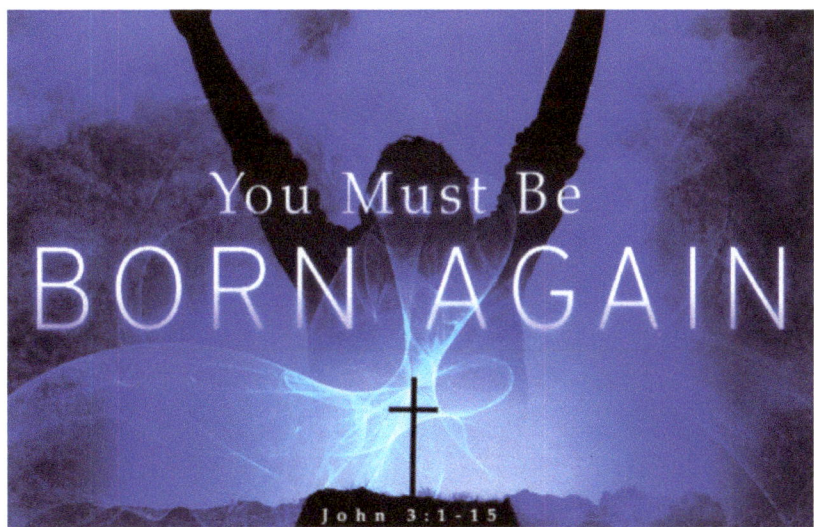

Bibliography

Coulter, Fred R., The Appointed Times of Jesus the Messiah, York Publishing Company, PO Box 1038, Hollister, California, 95024-1038

Coulter, Fred R., The Day That Jesus the Christ Died, York Publishing Company, PO Box 1038, Hollister, California, 95024-1038

Dake, Finis J., Dake's Annotated Reference Bible, Dake Bible Sales, P.O. Box 1050, Lawrenceville, Ga., 30246

Finegan, Jack, Handbook of Biblical Chronology, Hendrickson Publishing Company, Peabody, Ma.

Good, Joseph, Rosh Hashanah, and the Messianic Kingdom to Come, Hatikva Ministries, PO Box 3125, Port Arthur, Texas 77643-0703

Horn H. S. and L. H. Wood, The Chronology of Ezra, TEACH Services, Inc., www.teachservices.com

Larkin, Clarence, Dispensational Truth, P.O. Box 334, Glenside, Pa., 1920

Logos apostolic Church of God and Bible College, Interlinear Greek and Hebrew Translation, Logos apostolic.org, United Kingdom, Logos apostolic.org

Nee, Watchman, Come Lord Jesus, Christian Fellowship Publishers, Inc., 11515 Allecingie Parkway, Richmond, Virginia 23235

Phillips, Don T., The Book of Revelation: *Mysteries Revealed*, 2nd Edition, Virtual Bookworm. com, PO Box 9949, College Station, Tx 77845

Phillips, Don T., The Book of Ruth: *Historical and Prophetic Truths*, Virtual Bookworm. com, PO Box 9949, College Station, Tx, 77845

Phillips, Don T., Life After Death: *Mysteries Revealed*, Virtual Bookworm. com, PO Box 9949, College Station, Tx, 77845

Phillips, Don T., The Eternal Plan of God: *Dispensations, Covenant Promises, Salvation*, Virtual Bookworm. com, PO Box 9949, College Station, Texas 7784.

Phillips, Don T., *The Birth and Death of Christ*, Virtual Bookworm. com, PO Box 9949, College Station, Tx, 77845

Phillips, Don T., The Book of Exodus: *Historical and Prophetic Truths* Virtual Bookworm. com, PO Box 9949, College Station, Tx, 77845

Phillips, Don T., A Biblical Chronology from Adam to Christ, Virtual Bookworm. com, PO Box 9949, College Station, Tx, 77845

Phillips, Don T., Life After the Great Tribulation: *The Millennial Kingdom,* Virtual Bookworm. com, PO Box 9949, College Station, Tx, 77845

Phillips, Don T., The Last 50 Days of Jesus Christ Virtual Bookworm. com, PO Box 9949, College Station, Tx, 77845

Phillips, Don T., The Daniel 70 Week Prophecy Virtual Bookworm. com, PO Box 9949, College Station, Texas 77845

Phillips, Don T., The Day of the Lord Virtual Bookworm. com, PO Box 9949, College Station, Texas 77845

Phillips, Don T., The Birth of Christ: *A Forensic Analysis of the Birth of Jesus Christ*
  Virtual Bookworm. com, PO Box 9949, College Station, Tx, 77845

Phillips, Don T., The Wrath and Judgments of God
  Virtual Bookworm. com, PO Box 9949, College Station, Texas 77845

Phillips, Don T., Biblical Truths about Difficult Concepts
  Virtual Bookworm. com, PO Box 9949, College Station, Texas 77845

Phillips, Don T., A New Pre-Wrath Rapture Theory
  Virtual Bookworm. com, PO Box 9949, College Station, Texas 77845

Phillips, Don T., The Olivet Discourse: Christ Speaks of His Second Coming, Virtual Bookworm. com, PO Box 9949, College Station, Texas 77845

Phillips, Don T., Rapture and Resurrection: The Blessed Hope of All Believers, Virtual Bookworm. com, PO Box 9949, College Station, Texas 77845

Phillips, Don T., The 7 Feasts of Israel, Virtual Bookworm. com, PO Box 9949, College Station, Texas 7784

Rosenthal, Matthew, The Pre-Wrath Rapture of the Church, Thomas Nelson Publishers, Nashville, Tennessee

Ryrie, Charles C., The Ryrie Study Bible, King James Version, Moody Press, Chicago. Ill

Salerno, Donald A., Revelation Unsealed, Virtual Bookworm.Com, P.O. Box 9949, College Station, Texas, 77842

Thiele, Edwin R., The Mysterious Numbers of the Hebrew Kings: *Revised Edition*, Kregel, Grand Rapids, Michigan

Thomas, Robert L., Revelation 1-7, An Exegetical Commentary, Moody Press, Chicago, Illinois

Thomas, Robert L., Revelation 8-22, An Exegetical Commentary, Moody Press, Chicago, Illinois

Van Kampen, Robert, The Sign, Crossway Books, 1300 Crescent Street, Wheaton, Illinois 60187

Walvoord, John F., The Millennial Kingdom, Academic Books, Zondervan Publishing Company, 1415 Lake Drive S.E., Grand Rapids, Michigan 49506

Footnote: This manuscript has drawn upon several excellent websites found by GOOGLE search. It is my intention to recognize every biblical scholar and source of information from those *giants that walked before me*. This information was sometimes not made available. In other cases, information was marked open source or not marked at all. If any author(s) sees any material that they want referenced, please contact me and I will acknowledge their previous research and scholarly work. In any case, I am extremely grateful for previous investigations or conclusions that may (or may not) support this work. God will know them and He will know the source.

Don T. Phillips
Senior Author

www.ingramcontent.com/pod-product-compliance
Lightning Source LLC
Chambersburg PA
CBHW060950170426
43202CB00026B/2997